PULAYATHARA

PAUL CHIRAKKARODE

PULAYATHARA

Translated from Malayalam by

CATHERINE THANKAMMA

edited by

MINI KRISHNAN

OXFORD
UNIVERSITY PRESS

OXFORD
UNIVERSITY PRESS

Oxford University Press is a department of the University of Oxford. It furthers the University's objective of excellence in research, scholarship, and education by publishing worldwide. Oxford is a registered trademark of Oxford University Press in the UK and in certain other countries.

Published in India by
Oxford University Press
2/11 Ground Floor, Ansari Road, Daryaganj, New Delhi 110 002, India

First Edition published in 2019

ISBN-13 (print edition): 978-0-19-949143-8
ISBN-10 (print edition): 0-19-949143-7

ISBN-13 (eBook): 978-0-19-909612-1
ISBN-10 (eBook): 0-19-909612-0

Typeset in Berling LT Std 10/15
by Tranistics Data Technologies, Kolkata 700 091
Printed in India by Replika Press Pvt. Ltd

Contents

Introduction

Catherine Thankamma

Home is not just a place of habitation. It is an idea, a concept deeply embedded in our collective unconscious ever since human beings gave up a nomadic way of life for a settled one. The idea of home is one that simultaneously represents physiological, psychological, and social needs. The Malayalam word *thara* can variously mean floor, platform, foundation, and home. For the Pulayar and Parayar, two Dalit castes of Kerala, *thara* was often a 36-square-foot raised mud platform enclosed by a framework made by binding together whole/slit bamboo poles and thick ribs of coconut branches, the walls and roof covered with woven coconut sheaves. To this they would return after the day's hard labour, to rest their aching bones till dawn. For these repressed people—who hardly had any aspirations and which, if they dared to have any, were hardly ever realized—*thara* should have been an asylum, a sanctuary. However, in the caste-determined feudalistic social fabric, even the surety of a home was denied to the so-called untouchable castes. *Pulayathara* (1962) depicts how the socially sanctioned substantive inequality that existed in nineteenth-century Kerala turned 'home' into a site of oppression and subjugation.

Social inequality and compartmentalization of human beings into groups of 'privileged' and 'the other' have marked human interaction in all societies at all times. However, inequality and segregation based on caste is endemic to the Indian social reality. Two defining features of caste-based stratification of society are as follows: membership is endogamous and social mobility is impossible. Christianity is thought to have arrived in Kerala in the 6th century CE through the Syrian traders.

It was quite amorphous at that time. The later schisms within the Kerala Church, the believers being separated as Syrian Christians and Syrian Catholics, and the origin of the Latin Catholic Church can all be traced to the arrival of the Portuguese in 15th century CE. Later on, active proselytizing work done by British missionaries, particularly among Dalits and tribal people, led to the spread of the Anglican faith. Christianity in Kerala, however, followed a different trajectory. The advent of Christianity in Kerala can be traced to its centuries-old maritime relations with lands along the Mediterranean coast such as Egypt, Tyre, Rome, Jerusalem, and Syria. Many of the Syrian traders were members of the Eastern Church. Some of them may have married local women and settled down in Kerala. Their descendants came to be called Syrian Christians as they followed the Syrian liturgical rites. The Syrian Christians also called themselves St Thomas Christians, tracing the origin of their faith to the evangelism of the apostle St Thomas in the first century, supposedly among the Namboothiris (Kerala Brahmins). There is no factual/historical basis for this claim, and the fact of the apostle's landing on the Kerala coast has been refuted by the Vatican. In all probability the Syrian Christians' claim to upper-caste status originated from the grants of land and various other privileges given to Syrian traders by the local chieftains who actively encouraged maritime trade and patronized the Syrian, Arab, and Jewish traders who landed on their shores. Since these ethnic groups were situated outside the *varna* system, they were not bound by its prescriptive norms. At the same time the granting of land and other privileges—as evidenced by the Jewish copper plates in the synagogue in Mattanchery (1000 CE) and the Tharisappalli copper plates (849 CE) awarded by the Chera ruler of Venad to the Syrian traders—enabled their descendants to become landlords and claim upper-caste status, a claim largely uncontested by the high-caste Hindu population. Though later various schisms led to the emergence of multiple sects within the Syrian Christian community, one commonality remained: they all claimed upper-caste status, a status that they denied to those who converted to Christianity during the second phase of conversion under the Portuguese. As mentioned earlier the British missionaries targeted Dalits and tribals, but they also worked hard for the uplift of economically backward classes and castes. If Benjamin Bailey, who was appointed to the Kottayam mission, translated the Bible to Malayalam, institutions such as C.M.S. College, Kottayam, validated the sincere and dedicated work of the early missionaries. Many Dalits converted to Christianity as this ensured food, shelter, and education. However, the Syrian Christians resented the conversion of Dalits and tribals, and this led to the emergence of two distinct groups—the Syrian Christians, who called themselves upper-caste 'ancient Christians', and the newly converted Dalit Christians, referred to as *avasha kristyanikal*[1] or *puthu kristyanikal*.[2] It is ironic that even a monotheistic religion such as Christianity, which promised brotherhood, became mired in the stifling hold of caste.

Born as the son of Rev. L.T. Daniel, a first-generation Dalit convert and preacher of the Christian Missionary Society, Paul Chirakkarode (1938–2008) could be called privileged in the sense that he had access to education. This, in turn, heightened his consciousness of the humiliation and suffering of the poor, oppressed, disenfranchised sections of society, especially his own community, and engendered in him an almost evangelical zeal for justice, which can be seen even in his early writings. It is no accident that he graduated in law and got a master's degree in English and Malayalam literature. Two great influences in his life during this period were B.R. Ambedkar

[1] Low-caste or depressed Christians. The term was often used in a derogatory sense to refer to newly converted Christians.

[2] Newly-converted Christians. The term was used to refer to those who converted to Christianity in the eighteenth and nineteenth centuries.

and communism. Chirakkarode soon emerged as a social activist and a prolific writer who authored a substantial body of work, which includes novels, biographies, several collections of short stories, as well as critical articles on a wide range of subjects. His biography of B.R. Ambedkar (*Ambedkar: Blazing Buddhist Agitation, a Study*, Dalit Books: Thiruvalla, 1993) is a monumental work.

Pulayathara has a simple storyline. What makes it unique is that it is the earliest literary narrative that records the debilitating complexities of Dalit Christian experience and the hollowness of religious conversion in Kerala's caste-ridden society. It is undocumented history, history from the margins. Though the novel focuses on the exploitation and marginalization of Dalit Christians, the plight of indigenous Dalits is depicted with equal sensitivity. At the start of the novel, the Dalit world is set against the feudal, agrarian backdrop of the Kuttanad region of central Kerala, which has the lowest altitude in the Indian peninsula, and where paddy fields were created by reclaiming the backwaters, mainly the Vembanad Kayal (lake). These reclamations were called *padasekaram*, groups of fields. As the fields were below sea level, brackish water from the backwaters flooding the crop was a constant fear that haunted landowner and labourer alike. When that happened, the labourers bailed out the fields using water wheels called *chakram*. According to the social formations of nineteenth-century Kerala, the landowners were either upper-caste Hindus or wealthy Syrian Christians. The ones who worked on the land were Pulayar and Parayar. Paradoxically, while their labour was central to the agrarian socio-economic structure, their untouchable status relegated them to the periphery of society. They did not own land. For instance, though Thevan Pulayan himself builds up the land on which his six-pole shack stands, by reclaiming the backwaters, he cannot claim it as his own. His brief mistaken sense of ownership is shattered when the landlord installs another labourer in the hut he called home. The converts who are allowed to build homes on land owned by the Church are haunted by the same sense of vulnerability. In such a context, the idea of the home as an asylum gets subverted. For both groups, home does not signify security; it heightens their awareness of the tenuous nature of their ownership. Again, whether it is the row of huts constructed along the outer edge of the fields bordering the backwaters or the homes of the converts that stand on Church land, these domiciles are restricted to a definite space, a kind of ghetto, well away from the homes of the upper-caste Hindu and Christian landlords.

The novel powerfully illustrates the link between language and empowerment and as a means of hegemonic assertion. It is seen everywhere, from names to sermons. Preacher Stephen's artful use of words from the Gospel, 'Look at the birds of the air', is a brilliant example of manipulating language to ensure compliance. Pallithara Pathros is so filled with a sense of exaltation that he forgets his earlier bitterness:

> Christ would wipe away his tears. Like the bridegroom who holds his virgin bride close to his chest, Christ will embrace him. At that time his dark-skinned body would be transformed into a rose-tinted one. He sat smiling as though he actually saw the transformation and the heavenly Canaan[3] in his mind.

The insidiousness of cultural conditioning that has him envisioning himself as rose-tinted is noteworthy. While the voice of the omniscient narrator follows a different register—incisive, echoing biblical cadences—the monosyllabic utterances and half-sentences that mark the responses of the low castes powerfully illustrate the connection between the denial of subjectivity and silencing of voices. Even when thoughts crowd their minds, men such as Thevan and Kali Parayan remain mute or fumble helplessly for words. Even Paulos is frustrated by his inability to express himself clearly.

[3] According to the Old Testament of the Bible, Jehovah made a covenant with Abraham to grant the land of Canaan to his descendants, the Jews. Canaan thus became the 'promised land.'

Significantly, centuries of silent submission has inured the Dalit to muteness to such a degree that he views the ability to speak as amazing. Hearing Outha Pulayan speak, Pallithara Pathros is reminded of the biblical story where Balaam's donkey received the power of speech. The novel ends with the Dalits' tentative steps towards self-articulation and affirmation of identity.

Pulayathara is not just a protest. The narration of the Pulayars' selfless labour, their almost umbilical relationship with the soil, their innate musical heritage, culture, and traditions, make it a life-affirming celebration of Dalit identity. This enables the novel to transcend its historical space to become a literary work that marks a major thematic and stylistic break from canonical upper-caste writing by providing an alternate aesthetic rooted in authentic, vibrant, felt experience.

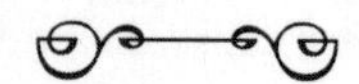

1

The Field of a Thousand Measures of Paddy

The month of Makaram, the time when emerald paddy saplings break through the soil. There is a channel in the middle of the *padasekaram*, the cluster of fields. When the rays of the sun fall on it, it glitters like a silver hip-chain. Water drawn from it has to irrigate all the fields in the month of Makaram.

Fissures appeared, cracking the dried fields. The green sheaves of the paddy plants grew pale and drooped. It seemed there would be no rain that year either. Not even a sliver of a dark cloud could be seen in the sky. White cloudlets floated across the deep blue sky like the wind-swept beard-grass seed.

Thevan Pulayan[1] came to the edge of the field and gazed at the crop. A basket of fire flared within the old Pulayan's chest. The scene was unbearable. For the past sixty years, Thevan Pulayan had been harvesting those fields. Not once had the crop failed. Neither worms nor flying pests had damaged the crop. As a head Pulayan people respected Thevan Pulayan. The local folk said, 'Thevan Pulayan lives for those fields.'

[1] A caste considered untouchable. Caste was as much a marker of identity as name and was suffixed to it. The name could be omitted, but the caste name hardly ever was. While 'Pulayar' was used to refer to members of the caste and the caste as a whole, the individual male carried the tag 'Pulayan' with his name. Polen'e and Pelen'e are vocatives of the word Pulayan. Pelayan and Pelen are unsophisticated variants of Pulayan.

That was true. Night and day, the head Pulayan could be seen in some corner of the cluster of fields. His thin body moved like the tear of a dark shadow. The elder landlord would stand beyond the outer fence in the shade of some coconut tree holding a woven palm-leaf umbrella over his head, watching. Thevan would either be working on the embankment, strengthening it, or making a sluice in the bund for water to flow. It was as though the man needed no rest. What tireless vigour! You could see his eyes gleaming with enthusiasm when he reached the field.

An outer fence, where wild pandanus bushes grew thickly, formed the boundary of the field. The path to the fields also lay along the outer fence. If you walked along that path, you could see the fields owned by the other landlords. Their crops were barely half grown. But the crop in Aayirampara[2] field grew thick and rich, and as tall as a man, blocking your sight. One could easily hide behind the thick dark broad leaves. People would stand on the embankment and say, 'That land is Narayanan Nair's. It is Thevan Pulayan who works in that field.'

'Which Thevan Pulayan?'

'Don't you know? Thevan Pulayan of Anjilthara.'

That was how the people in that land knew Narayanan Nair, the owner of Aayirampara field, a matter which pleased Narayanan Nair. If Thevan Pulayan gathered a fistful of grain and scattered it, there would be an explosion of seedlings. The harvest would be ten measures more than in any other plot. The dark-skinned women who harvested the crop felt their arms ache with all the reaping. Their menfolk too found it difficult to carry the bundles of paddy to the threshing yard. There the paddy would lie in a mountain-like heap. Narayanan Nair felt proud as he watched the pile of golden grain. He would think, 'God has been gracious this year as well. There will be no shortages.'

[2] *Aayiram* means a thousand; *para* means a measure equal to three kilograms.

The landlord recalled the time Thevan Pulayan had first come to work there. It was during an Onam and the seasonal work was going on. Thevan, a dark sprightly boy, came along with the elder Pulayan of that time. Narayanan Nair was reclining on a cot made of woven cane next to the granary. Deep inside, he felt a strange interest in the boy with the rock-dark skin. As he smeared lime on a cool betel leaf, he asked in a voice that echoed like a conch shell, 'Who is this boy?'

'He is from this lowly one's community, Tham'ra,'[3] the elder Pulayan answered respectfully.

'Hmm,' Narayanan Nair grunted deeply. The fiery red eyes of that imposing man ran over the boy's ink-black body. 'Would you like to start work here, boy?'

'O,' came the humble response.

That was how Thevan Pulayan joined that year's Onam-related work in Narayanan Nair's field. There were other workers in the great house at that time. Thevan Pulayan went along with them to the field. Even today, the memory of that first sight of Aayirampara field was fresh in his memory. Astonishing beyond measure! Nothing in his life could equal that wondrous sight. The field stretched out before him, a broad green expanse that seemed to reach the gateway of the horizon. Kuttanad's endless stretch of green filled Thevan Pulayan with awe. He had seen fields before, tiny bits of land trapped between hills. The vastness of the Kuttanadan fields bewildered him.

'Acho,'[4] he called the elder Pulayan. 'All these fields that we see, it is our people who work on them, isn't it?'

The elder Pulayan did not think that the question had any great significance. Who other than the Pulayar worked in the field? Only

[3] Abbreviated form of *thampuran,* meaning lord/master. *Tham'ra* is its variant. It is ironical that *thampuran* refers to both god and landlord.

[4] Variant of father/priest, as per the context. Other variants are *achan, acha, acho,* and *achen.*

a Pulayan could work in water and clay without thought of night and day. There were farmers from other communities too. They too gathered fistfuls of grain to scatter across the field. But to see a field that was sown and watered by a Pulayan was a festival for the eyes. Streams of his sweat had to fall on the clay. If they fell, they too became a fertilizer. The air he exhaled had to stroke the sheaves of the plant. If it did, it made the crop flourish. All these were such strong magical forces.

Very soon, Thevan Pulayan made a name for himself as a labourer. However chilly it was, he did not hesitate to go out to work. That dark-skinned body brimmed with health. A large frame that seemed to say, 'Let me work.' In those days, there were just four shacks on the northern edge of Narayanan Nair's field. Thevan needed a place to live. For the time being, he decided to stay in each of the four shacks alternately.

In this manner, Thevan started to work. At midnight, the Pulayan would push the boat meant to carry clay into the backwaters and ply it across the vast expanse. Alone. In the milky white of the moonlit Makaram sky, boat and boatman could be seen moving like a black shadow. Just before daybreak, the boat would reach the outer fence laden with clay. In a month's time, he had built up a firm landmass that could support a shack built around six bamboo poles. He built a boundary with the thick stalk of coconut leaves and bamboo. That evening, as he descended the steps, having collecting the day's wage of two measures of grain in the corner of the clay-smeared cloth tied around his waist, Thevan Pulayan said, 'Tham'ra, this lowly one has made a landmass near the outer fence.'

'*Hmm*.' Narayanan Nair grunted. The fiery-red eyes became even more intense. He looked him over once, then asked, 'Have you levelled it?'

'It is done, Tham'ra.'

'*Hmm*. All right. You can build your home,' Thampuran gave his permission. His heart full of gratitude, Thevan was about to step across the roofed gateway when Thampuran asked, 'Do you have bamboo and coconut leaves?'

Thevan's head sank forward. Helplessness shrouded his heart. That man, who worked hard every day of his life, did not have the means to build a house. There was something piteous in his stance!

'I will give you bamboo and palm leaves. In return I'll take twenty measures of paddy at the time of harvest. Remember that. Are you willing?'

Thevan Pulayan trembled. The tremor seemed to shake every nerve in his body. Thampuran would take twenty measures of paddy at harvest time! What remained after that would be the payment for his labour. The Kuttanadan Pulayan was in debt year after year. He had a ready-to-use reply for all his creditors: 'When harvest comes, Tham'ra.' If he lost twenty measures at that time, many plans would go wrong.

'Yes, I will, Tham'ra. I'm willing,' Thevan Pulayan said, sighing deeply.

The glow of unshed tears hovered on his tired lashes as Thevan said this. His eyes became moist, sobs rose in his throat, but he controlled himself. Whatever the loss, he would be gaining a home that he could claim as his own. That was not a small thing, was it? Indeed, it was a great achievement! The six-pole *thara*[5] that was taking shape was part of a beautiful dream. Its details sent a thrill along his body. He would marry a girl, dark-skinned like himself, in the presence of his community. Accompanied by a procession of people, walking under a silken umbrella, with drum beats and piped music, he would arrive and begin his life in that home. Thevan wanted to enter life in that manner. Would all those dreams come true?

[5] Can variously mean platform, base, floor, and home. In the course of the novel, what begins as a home ends up as a ghetto. This makes the word *thara* and the title *Pulayathara* highly nuanced.

Soon a new shack could be seen on the well-beaten and levelled land, next to the four shacks. Thevan shifted to Anjilthara, the fifth shack. On that occasion he served his people beaten and puffed rice. Toddy, too, was served on a modest scale.

Everyone chewed betel, spat the juice, and left. Night had fallen. Thevan spread a woven-leaf mat on the floor and lay down to sleep, but sleep evaded him. An overpowering loneliness filled his heart. That night Thevan longed for a companion in his life. A month later he got married. Chirutha was good to look at. She was also a capable labourer. Once she entered the field at dawn, she would reap a hundred or hundred and fifty sheaves, thereby giving no room for complaint. Thevan rejoiced in getting such a partner.

Memories unfurled one after the other in his mind as Thevan Pulayan stood in the scorching heat and looked at the field. He could see the stream that shimmered like a silver hip-chain. On both sides he could see boats and wheels in the fields. Somewhere far away he could make out figures plying the wheel, pouring cool water at the roots of the parched plants, a pious act!

'My Tham'ra alone has not fixed either wheel or boat,' thought Thevan Pulayan.

If neither boat nor wheel was used to water the paddy, the crop would dry up. The drought was that severe. Thevan Pulayan felt very weak. Strength and vitality had long since disappeared from under his wrinkled skin. He no longer had his old enthusiasm or vigour. Nothing excited him anymore. He had reached a stage where he could not even sing the songs usually sung while plying the wheel. Total apathy.

Thevan Pulayan walked towards Anjilthara. He must send his son Kandankoran to the fields. The boy had no sense of responsibility. What would his life be if he continued in this manner? All Kandankoran did was play cards with the wastrels who gathered under the shade of coconut palms. Thevan Pulayan said to himself, 'It's my son after all who must continue this work.'

As Thevan Pulayan walked along the outer fence, he saw the elder landlord coming towards him from the opposite direction holding a woven umbrella. The Pulayan drew back to the very edge and stood respectfully, head bowed. The man's humble posture seemed to have pleased Thampuran. Narayanan Nair straightened his second cloth and asked, 'Shouldn't you draw water, Thevan Polen'e?'

'I should, Tham'ra.'

'Then why don't you bring the wheel, boat, and whatever else you need, and start drawing water?' Thampuran's words sounded like a rebuke. Each word held the heat of a glowing ember. Thevan Pulayan felt singed. He was losing the good name he had earned as an efficient worker. That he had waited for Thampuran to say it before he got out the wheel and erected the spokes to draw water—how disgraceful!

Thampuran asked, 'Where is your son, that useless Kandankoran?'

Thevan Pulayan felt a searing pain in his heart. Kandankoran was his son. A son whom he had brought up by working hard, digging deep in the mire. He might be lazy, he might lack a sense of responsibility, but it was he who had given meaning to Thevan Pulayan's life. When unending labour piled up before his eyes, it was the thought that he was working for his son that brought him comfort. There was a sense of satisfaction in it. It was Kandankoran who had given him that satisfaction. It was only when he thought of Kandankoran that Thevan experienced the numbness of something tightening around the navel; that was because he was a father! Thampuran had called him a wastrel. Thampuran's son was a drunkard and a womanizer—no, he could not say all that. If it was anyone else he could have said something.

'Didn't you hear me ask? Where is your son?' Thampuran's voice rose.

'He's in our *thara*.'

'What work does he do? Climbs coconut trees, steals, and squanders; isn't that true?'

That sentence, too, pierced Thevan Pulayan's heart like a twirling chisel. Thampuran ordered, 'You and your son should erect the wheel and start plying it today itself, you hear me?'

'O,' Thevan replied humbly.

A labourer was not supposed to think for himself. Even if he did, he could not say it aloud. It was forbidden. When Thampuran decided, the worker murmured his assent. That was how it had been for generations.

Thampuran walked away. He had gone some distance when he turned and said, 'Have your morning meal from my house.'

'O.' Again the humble assent.

Thampuran's palm leaf umbrella moved farther and farther away. Thevan stood watching it. He felt a terrible ache in his heart, as though something heavy was weighing it down. He felt breathless. Thampuran felt no affection for his Kandankoran. It was possible that the next-generation worker would rise against the landlord. Would that be the beginning of a struggle?

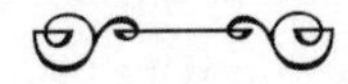

2
Cracks Appear

Night. Moonlight spread abundantly everywhere, milk-like. The fields looked beautiful. Thevan Pulayan sat firmly on the wooden frame and began to sing the song that accompanied the plying of the wheel in the fields:

Tilled in the channel, removed some sludge
Then stood at the fence for wages …

Waves of song spread farther and farther, crossing the sublime silence of the night. The very field thrilled with joy. In that tiny world of labour, the labourer sang his heart out to prevent himself from falling asleep, to forget the hardship of his work. The attractive verses grew increasingly louder. A young man's song merged with it to flow as one. It was Kandankoran's voice. At that moment the folk song gained a life of its own. It was creating a beautiful world, one without artifice, where there was only selfless labour.

The wheel with seven blades continued to turn. At each turn water splashed into the field. At that time, too, the song rose and continued to flow, filling the expanse of Aayirampara field and beyond. That living song that poured profusely from the Kuttanadan Pulayan's throat!

In a building far away, Raghava Kurup who was listening to the radio said, 'Pulayan is plying the wheel.'

When Narayanan Nair entered the room, his son stood up respectfully.

'Turn off that song box, will you?'

The son obeyed. Waves of song from the *punjapadam*, the paddy field, continued to flow across the quiet sky. That song the exhausted labourer sang to forget the pain of hard work had its own soul. Father and son heard it together. Narayanan Nair ran his fingers through the hair on his chest and asked, 'Did you go to the outer fence?'

'I did.'

'And?'

'Many coconuts are missing. At least a hundred.' Raghava Kurup then continued to report the theft. They had been cut by the bunch. If things continued in this manner it would be terrible, he said. This has been going on for some time. The coconut palms near the outer fence have a good yield. But they, the owners, have not yet had the opportunity to enjoy that yield.

Narayanan Nair looked at his son, his fiery eyes bulging. 'Do you know who the thief is?'

Raghava Kurup's reply came like an arrow. 'Who else? That Kandankoran.'

Raghava Kurup had proof. Not one, many. Kandankoran walked around grandly, fresh from his bath, forehead smeared with coloured powder, his curly hair neatly patted into place, wearing a printed dhoti that reached his feet. He was never short of money. You should see him throwing coins when he makes a bid at cards! He is never without a packet of twenty-five *beedis*, rolled betel leaves with bits of tobacco inside, and a card-mark matchbox. From where does he get all this money?

Narayanan Nair sat with bowed head as though sunk in thought. He was facing a grave problem. He could not pluck out Thevan Pulayan from the group of workers attached to that great house and send him away. It was not right. When Thevan Pulayan joined the house as a labourer the family home was just an old building. There were a couple of oxen, a huge haystack, and a thriving crop of *kudivazha* plantains. It was only after Thevan had started to work there that the land began to flourish. These days one could not see through the lush green yard. Abundance flourished and multiplied beautifully all around him. Thevan Pulayan had made it all happen. Now those hands had grown weak. But one could not forget the long, long years of enduring loyalty.

'Kandankoran cannot be allowed to live in Anjilthara. He is insolent,' said Raghava Kurup.

Once again Narayanan Nair lowered his head. Additions and subtractions, shedding and measuring, went on in his heart. He still remembered how Anjilthara had taken shape, how Thevan Pulayan had built up that levelled land by bringing a boat-full of clay every night. Without much delay a hut had been built. So many years had gone by since then. Thevan Pulayan began his life there with a lot of expectations. Thevan had just one thought. He should see Thampuran prosper. Now, when their children had grown up, were confrontations beginning?

'He shows absolutely no respect for his social superiors,' Raghava Kurup continued. 'He won't even acknowledge my presence.' Anger flared. He said through clenched teeth, 'He is insolent.'

Narayanan Nair shared that opinion. Kandankoran went about with his shoulders straight, chest stuck out, his curly hair smoothly swept backward, his coloured dhoti reaching his feet. There was always a glowing *beedi* between his lips. He showed no deference even when he saw Thampuran walking briskly in his direction. All these were signs of an insolent man, were they not?

'But Thevan Pulayan is a harmless soul. I am not able to do anything when I think of the old Pulayan.'

Raghava Kurup agreed. Thevan was his father's trustworthy servant. He had often seen the old Pulayan standing in the customary humble posture before his father; a father who could tame his servants and keep them in line. He, Raghava Kurup, was the son of that capable Narayanan Nair. He, too, wanted to exercise control, hammer the labourers into submission, and make them obey him. He, Raghava Kurup, had his father's blood in his veins. It was potent. The time had come for the new generation to take over authority from the older one. Would Kandankoran submit to Raghava Kurup's control?

At the time this exchange was taking place between father and son in a room in the great house, far away in the paddy field Thevan and Kandankoran were plying the wheel, their song floating clearly in the air. Muddy water flowed from the channel into the field.

A cool breeze was blowing, pressing forward over the moonlit paddy field. Thevan Pulayan was on the top step of the wheel. Kandankoran sat on the one below. The wheel had fourteen blades. It required the hard labour of two able-bodied men to ply the wheel and make it turn. There were calluses on Thevan Pulayan's feet, formed from years of standing firmly on the blades. Kandankoran was still getting used to the work, having wandered about idly all these years. But could he get out of that mire-filled field and lead a different life?

The next day Thampuran arrived at the edge of the field. The sight brought a sparkle to his eyes. Thickly growing paddy stood neck-deep in water. Thevan Pulayan stood in one corner of the field like a shadow.

The Pulayan approached Thampuran and said, 'Tham'ra, it would be nice if we could sprinkle some fertilizer now.'

'Why not? Let it be done,' Narayanan Nair agreed. Thevan Pulayan crouched down to gather rubbish and heap it against the ridge. Thampuran stood watching for a while. Finally he issued a direction, 'Thevan Polen'e, see that the bund does not collapse. Don't say I didn't warn you.'

'O.'

Thampuran left, shaking his woven umbrella as he walked. Thevan Pulayan went and stood on the ridge at the southern boundary. Huge pandanus palms grew thickly on that ridge. It was wise to have the *pula* palms with their crown of fruit growing there. Even the mightiest wave that swirled and crashed against the bund could not damage them. However, Thevan Pulayan could not control a sense of unease. On one side was the beautifully decked paddy field ready for harvest. On the other side lay the backwaters, stretching till eternity. Waves rose and fell at all times, striking fiercely against the barrier. How long could the narrow barrier ridge protect the fields?

All at once Thevan exclaimed, calling on his family deity, '*Ente paratheive*! Have you abandoned us?'

A tiny hole had appeared on the outer ridge. Crabs often made such holes scratching endlessly with their claws. Brackish water from the backwaters was oozing through the hole. The hole was a tiny one. But could a responsible elder Pulayan pretend not to have seen it? At the speed of wind, the brackish water could very well pour in and create a breach. Frightened, Thevan Pulayan unconsciously placed his hand upon his heart. 'That has to be plugged and made firm.'

The backwaters roared as though in a mood to destroy everything. Huge waves rocked and crashed on the water. They pounded the outer fence, leaving behind a frothy mark. The dense growth of pandanus palms with their thorny crowns shook violently as each wave struck them.

Thevan Pulayan felt his feet grow heavy. Even as he walked they seemed not to move. As soon as he reached home he would get Kandankoran and take the clay boat across the backwaters. With one boat load of clay he should be able to fill the hole. He could then make it firm with hay, plant waste, and whatever rubbish he could find. Anxiety began to fill Thevan Pulayan's heart. Drops of sweat appeared on his wrinkled face.

When he reached Anjilthara there was no one inside. Kandankoran had gone off somewhere. Thevan Pulayan stood in front of the empty house and let out a call in the distance, '*Eda*[1] Kandankora, *pooee*!'

[1] A word used to address someone (masculine). *Da* or *edo* are used alternatively.

The anger that welled up within him resonated in that call. That call which emerged from the labourer's throat fell upon the emerald paddy saplings that had taken root in the Makaram fields and echoed. It went and struck the golden cloud-laden horizon far away, and resonated. Even after the call ended the echo seemed to reverberate in the air. Again the call rang out,

'Kandankora ... *pooee*!'

From somewhere far away came the son's answering call, '*Oyee*.'

'Come here.'

Thevan Pulayan waited. Quite some time must have gone by in that manner. When Kandankoran arrived he asked his father, 'Why did you call me, Appa?'[2]

Thevan looked at his son once all over. There was something unusual in that look. It was the look that directed an irresponsible wayward son towards the duties he needed to take on. Thevan Pulayan said, '*Eda* Kandankora, we need to repair that bund.'

Father and son got into the clay-loading boat and rowed out into the backwaters. The boat moved towards the farther bank. It would be late midnight when they returned. Then perhaps they might unload a boatload of clay on the embankment.

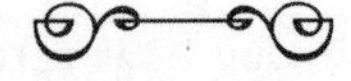

[2] Vocative of *appan*, meaning father.

3
Impasse

They rowed across the backwaters towards a place that was shallow, then dug the long bamboo pole into the floor and tied the boat to it. Thevan and Kandankoran stepped across the cross-planks into the water and began to dig up clay. The only sound to be heard was that of the waves.

The boat was almost full. Thevan Pulayan said, '*Eda* Kandankora, we'll move the boat a bit. There's no more clay here.'

They pushed the boat a little, then prepared to dive. Kandankoran said, 'Appa, you sit in the boat. I'll go and dig up the clay.'

Droplets of water dripping from his body, Thevan Pulayan climbed into the boat and sat on the footrest, bending double. Kandankoran dived, basket in hand, straight into the deep water. Bubbles of air rose from the floor. Now he must be digging up the settled clay with his hands. Such exhausting labour! Thevan Pulayan sat hunched on the foothold. After a while Kandankoran's head and a basket of clay rose above the water.

'Acho, I think it's going to rain.'

'*Ayyo*!' Thevan Pulayan exclaimed, looking up. Coal-black clouds were gathering into a thick mass. White forks of lightning flashed playfully across the dark sky. All of a sudden the backwaters began to roar and roll. Waves peaked like mountains. The wooden boat tilted and slid on the water, somehow managing to stay afloat.

Panicking, Thevan Pulayan shouted, 'Kandakora, get in quickly.' Kandankoran let go of the basket, but when in the blazing flashes of lightning he saw it move away over the waves, he tried to swim after it. Thevan Pulayan stopped him. 'Let it go, *k'datha*.'[1]

Kandankoran half swam, half floated on the roaring waves. Somehow he climbed into the boat and collapsed on the heap of clay. The boat rocked precariously on the waves, unable to stay still. Who could say when it would overturn? The rain and wind continued unabated even then. The bitter wind blew as though determined to destroy everything. Lightning danced across the boundless sky. Rolls of thunder hit the water and reverberated frighteningly.

For a moment, Thevan Pulayan stared at his son lying in a stupor on his side; then, sitting on the prow of the boat, he plunged the paddle forcefully into the water. The boat moved forward over the mounting waves slicing through them. The backwaters roared fearfully, but Thevan Pulayan did not lose courage. A little ahead could be seen the island lined with coconut trees. The boat had to go beyond the island to reach the northern edge of the field. Enough strength to achieve that goal awakened within him, enabling him to row.

'*Ente paratheive,* wonder what has become of the ridge by now!'

In the glare of the flashes of lightning, he saw the coconut tree-lined island. Strength surged into Thevan's veins. The paddle seemed insufficient for the Pulayan's hands. He felt he would reach nowhere if he rowed with it. But the boat was galloping forward. The waves tossed the boat this way and that. It did not matter even if the lumps of clay fell into the water; they should reach the bank alive. It began to rain heavily. The outer bund would surely have collapsed by now.

Rowing tirelessly for a long time, they at last reached the outer bund. Water was rushing into Aayirampara field. Unconsciously, Thevan beat his chest. His deity had forsaken him. Unable to withstand the onrush of the deluge, the tiny hole he had seen

[1] Son or boy. *K'dathan* or *kidathan* are variants.

during the day had caused the embankment to collapse. The *pula* palms that lined the ridge floated on the water, uprooted.

Kandankoran just stood and stared, motionless. To see his expressionless face, one would think he had expected such a catastrophe to happen! Thevan Pulayan broke down, weeping. The old labourer's heart was overcome. The uprooted paddy shoots in Aayirampara field must be lying submerged in the flood.

Thevan Pulayan lamented loudly as though his heart had broken, 'How will I go to my Tham'ra's house now?'

That year's crop had been destroyed completely. Even if he repaired the broken ridge, made it firm, and drained the water, it was doubtful whether the crop would thrive. Apart from all this, people would say that the elder Pulayan's irresponsibility had led the embankment to collapse. And was that not true? There had been a hole in the ridge. The labourer saw it, yet pretended not to.

A grievous failing!

Thevan Pulayan and Kandankoran mended the ridge, and made it firm before daybreak. They stopped the water from brimming over into the field; that much was done. Now they had to drain the water using four or five wheels. For that they had to ask Thampuran's permission. The wheels had to be taken from the wheel shed in Thampuran's grounds. They would need additional workers as well.

'What will my Tham'ra say?'

The harsh wind had blown and the heavy rain had fallen not because Thevan Pulayan ordered it. It just happened. And the weak bund collapsed. The next thing to be done was to dig and make it firm; that was the only remedy. It would cost quite a lot of money. The faithful Pulayan's heart ached at the huge loss his Thampuran would incur. He felt extremely repentant. However, Thevan Pulayan found it difficult to mould his tongue to utter these feelings. What if Thampuran became furious?

Water dripping down his head, Thevan Pulayan swam across the outer fence and walked along the ridge with hunched shoulders. There was clay and muck on that dark-skinned body. A torn, loosely woven towel lay scrunched up on his shoulder. Far away, through the outspread peacock feathers of the young coconut palms, through gaps in the green, he could see the whitewashed walls of Thampuran's ancestral house.

There was no one to be seen at the front of the house. The huge doors stood wide open, the curtain swaying gently. Thevan Pulayan did not have the right to approach the main doorway. The beautifully constructed steps that led to the door and the broad path thickly laid with silvery sand were forbidden to the poor labourer. Only the upper castes whose pot-bellies rolled and shook when they moved could walk along that path.

Thevan Pulayan paused doubtfully for a minute, then walked up the rough path strewn with rocks and thorns that lay towards the left. Only cattle were taken along that path.

Thevan Pulayan stood quietly in a corner of the yard. He saw Thampuratti's[2] face through the doorway. Like a lotus flower touched by the sun's rays, the beautiful face of the Goddess Lakshmi of that house looked out. A question.

'Thevan Pelen'e, when did you arrive?'

Thevan Pulayan said with great humility, 'This lowly one came just now, Tham'ratti.'

Narayanan Nair must have heard the conversation, for he came towards the kitchen. Thampuran saw the worker. Immediately his face became stern. It seemed as though sparks were flying from his fiery red eyes. 'You destroyed everything, didn't you, *eda*?' It was a roar. Thampuratti did not understand anything. Thevan Pulayan bowed his head in guilt.

Thampuran continued, 'I had warned you earlier to strengthen the bund. You didn't do it. You …' Unable to control his anger Thampuran gnashed his teeth. The labourer looked at him piteously. But that only seemed to kindle Thampuran's anger.

[2] Variant of *thampuratti*, meaning landlord's wife or high-caste woman.

Narayanan Nair asked, 'Why have you come now, after ruining everything?'

Thevan was struck dumb. Thampuran was pointing his finger at him. It was a serious accusation. The service of many years was being wiped out in a minute. It was due to Thevan Pulayan's unstinted labour that that family had prospered. Without recalling any of that, Thampuran's words were like a slap across Thevan's face.

'Will we get even a grain of rice from that field now?' Thampuran's anger was just beginning to boil. Censure sprouted and surfaced in his heart. Narayanan Nair recalled that the hole in the ridge had been a tiny one, and that Thevan Pulayan could easily have plugged it. As he thought about it, sparks of fury seemed to fly out of his eyes once again. He saw with his mind's eye the entire Aayirampara field reduced to a wasteland.

A glance at his face revealed the inner conflict in Thampuran's mind. The face appeared furious. Thevan moved to one corner of the yard, afraid that the burning eyes would turn him to ashes.

Thampuran asked again, 'Why have you come after ruining everything?'

Thevan wanted to say many things. Words jostled within him. Perhaps it was the intensity of emotion; he could not utter a word. The sound of the heavy rain of the previous night still echoed hard in his ears. Thevan Pulayan said humbly, 'Tham'ra, the hole can be repaired and the wheel used to drain the water. So …'

Narayanan Nair laughed aloud. Something fiendish echoed in that laugh. Without losing heart Thevan Pulayan said humbly, 'Me and my son don't want payment Tham'ra. Whatever I …'

Narayanan Nair stopped him once and for all by saying, 'I don't want to hear anything, didn't I tell you that? Ruined everything, and now you come with your excuses. Now I'll do whatever has to be done.'

There echoed a terrible majesty in those words. The majesty of a firm decision. Thevan Pulayan's face streamed with sweat. That anxious soul wiped his face with the clay-smeared towel on his shoulder. He wondered if strength was draining from his body, from every nerve in his body. He felt the urge to sit down. He had to. He sat bundled up in a corner of the yard near the cowshed. The low boughs of the jackfruit tree spread their shade over him.

Kuhoo kuhoo. The glossy black bird screeched as though mocking him. It spread its wings and flew off into the infinity above.

When Thevan looked up, Thampuran's face had disappeared from the doorway. Neither was Thampuratti's fair face to be seen. But that silvery voice echoed in the kitchen. Faint strains of it poured out into the yard.

There was no one around. Thevan waited a while longer. No movement at all. Finally, he stood up and with great difficulty, began to walk along the stony uneven path. The slanting rays of the sun kissed his hollow cheeks. Thevan walked, his head bowed low. Familiarity led his feet forward. Thevan continued to walk for some time. He felt a cool breeze against him. What? Where was he? Thevan stared, his eyes wide open. He had reached the edge of Aayirampara field. He leaned against a coconut tree, gazing at the paddy field filled with water. *Havoo*! A cool breeze was blowing. He felt some relief.

'Acha, why are you standing here?' Kandankoran stood in front of him and asked. From which direction had he come? Lost in thought, Thevan had not even heard him approach. The father looked at his son. Regret reflected in the depths of the young man's eyes; teardrops stood poised in the corners of his eyes, ready to fall. A question arose, unbidden, from the bottom of Thevan's heart. 'What is it, *k'datha*? Why are you crying?'

'Acha, some others have come to stay in our *thara*,' Kandankoran somehow managed to get that out. His voice broke. Thevan could not believe his ears. Another family in Anjilthara! Even imagining it was impossible. It was his hands that had given shape to Anjilthara. It was he who had gone out on the backwaters with the clay boat, diving down into the freezing water to dig up clay and bringing it to the outer fence, it was he who had built up enough earth for a house, and finally, with Thampuran's permission, built a house. The scenes rose in Thevan's memory. They flashed across his mind like frames in a motion picture. Thevan Pulayan saw each scene. He let out a deep sigh.

'*Ente paratheive* ...'

4
The Break

It was Kunjol and family who came to live in Anjilthara. Kunjol was Thevan Pulayan's friend. They were close friends. Indeed, they seemed to share a life. That was what hurt Thevan Pulayan most. It was Thevan who had held the silk umbrella over Kunjol on his wedding day. For some time now, Kunjol had been on bad terms with Thampuran. He, therefore, used to work for daily wages in fields owned by other landlords. Now the same Kunjol had come to live in the *thara* Thevan had built! Most unexpected. A wound that shattered Thevan completely.

Thevan could not control himself. Hot blood drummed in every nerve. He wanted to dash into the house, question Kunjol, throw out his pots and pans, and then—still seething with anger—laugh grotesquely.

'I … I'll just go there and come. I have something to ask …'

But by the time Thevan angrily kicked and pushed away the bamboo fence and stood in front of Anjilthara, his strength seemed to have drained away. He could not speak. He felt as though a burning piece of charcoal was stuck in his throat. He felt overwhelmed. He had never experienced anything like this before. Some other family was occupying his home, a heartbreaking sight. As soon as he reached there Thevan Pulayan called out panting, '*Eda* Kunjol'e!'

Wearing a palm-spathe cap, Kunjol stepped out of the shack. He paled when he saw his friend. His head fell forward guiltily. Kunjol had done something that should never be done to a friend. Every minute that he stood on that floor which had blossomed out of

Thevan's sweat was like standing on live coal. He somehow found the courage to ask, 'Why have you come?'

Thevan's pale face seemed to burn red. That terrible flush! It was frightening to look him in the face.

'Kunjol'e, what is this that you have done? Better than this would have been for you to thrust a knife into my chest.'

Thevan stopped, breathless. Despair, helplessness, vengeance filled his heart. Everything was on fire. He wanted to avenge himself on someone. That impulse could not be controlled. But against whom would that eternally sorrowful old man avenge himself? Did he have the strength or ability to do that? Could he say anything to this society that had rendered him helpless all round? His anguish made him unfit to do anything. So Thevan Pulayan did what any other helpless man does; he wept. His vengeance was turning into pain. Sobbing, he said, 'I'm a poor man. All I wanted was that my Tham'ra should prosper but …'

Wiping his streaming tears, that exhausted man began to walk. His feet faltered. He walked in a deluge of despair, like a hollow tree trunk bobbing on water. Before his eyes lay the emerald field. It was there that Thevan had spent all his life. In that clayey field, at the foot of the saplings, on the ridges that wound about like nerves, drops of his sweat had fallen everywhere. The worker had only one wish: that his Thampuran should prosper. The Pulayan worked in that field day and night, without rest. Thevan Pulayan had had the good fortune to see Thampuran prosper. But why had that good Thampuran forsaken him?

Thevan Pulayan inhaled as much as he could the cool breeze that caressed the paddy shoots in Aayirampara field. His narrow chest rose and fell as a deep sigh twisted within him. He no longer had the right to enter that field. Another Pulayan would come to water the crop. When the wheels turned again in the fields swathed by the Makaram moonlight's embrace, the folks around would no longer hear Thevan Pulayan's song. As he lay in his room in the great house, snuggling against his wife for the warmth of her breast,

Thampuran will not hear the beautiful song that Thevan sang for the field. Would Kunjol be able to sing that song aloud?

Thevan's eyes brimmed. From behind the veil of tears, the emerald lost its brilliance. Once again a deep sigh rose from within him. He walked forward, controlling himself. Just then Kunjol came from the other side and walked past him. As Thevan looked on, Kunjol walked along the ridge to the wheel. He settled himself firmly. Slowly, the wheel began to turn. Water began to pour through the sluice.

Thevan could not bear to watch. He felt as though Kunjol was seated on his chest, crushing him. He found it difficult to breathe. That oppressed man leaned against a coconut tree and watched Kunjol ply the wheel.

'Acho,' Kandankoran called from beside him. 'Acha, why are you standing here?'

The father looked at the son through weary eyes. 'Should I continue to live?' they seemed to ask. Thevan looked as though his whole life had been destroyed. As though the work of a lifetime had fallen to pieces due to momentary weakness. Was a new beginning possible? It was not.

'Don't we need a place to spend the night?'

Old Thevan Pulayan neither agreed nor disagreed. To look at him, it seemed the worn-out man had lost his power of speech. The old man who had lost his strength was admitting defeat to the younger generation brimming with strength. That defeated man was no longer capable of anything. His helplessness was being expressed through soundless language. Without saying anything, Thevan Pulayan blinked his lowered eyes. Kandankoran answered the question himself. 'Yes, we need a place to sleep tonight.'

Thevan Pulayan continued to stare like an idiot. His son's words had not sunk into that aged head. Perhaps no new idea would enter it.

Kandankoran cleared his throat and said, 'We'll go to our Pallithara Pathrochayan's house.'

The old man merely looked at his son questioningly. The son explained. They needed a place to spend the night. Thevan Pulayan had not been able to acquire even a tiny measure of land for himself. It was not because he had not worked hard; nor was it because he had wasted time sitting idly in his shack. The prevailing social norms did not allow it. The system where a labourer was denied his rights should change. When would that day dawn?

'Do we have a home here? No. That is why I said we'll go to Pallithara Pathrochayan's house.'

Thevan nodded. Pallithara Pathros was a distant relative of Thevan's. Pathros's six-pole shack stood on the southern side of the Mission Church. It stood on land called Mission land that belonged to the Hilltop Church, which stood on a beautiful, lone hill, bearing a cross on its forehead. The land had been acquired by foreign missionaries a long time ago. They had built the Church, paid for all the expenses. Standing against the beautiful background of lush green rural land, the Church seemed like a white lotus. The unhappy people living around the Church were those who had converted to the Christian faith. The tiny shacks of the baptized ones lay scattered around the Church. Pathros was a *puthu kristyani*, one of the new Christians.

It must be twenty years now since Pathros had settled on the land owned by the Church. Before that he had lived on the western island near the outer fence. At that time Pathros was a Hindu Pulayan named Kiliyan, Thevan recalled. Kiliyan married the daughter of Thevan's great uncle on the maternal side. But she was now no more. It was after her death that Kiliyan brought home Kunjazhaki. That was *illakkettu*, a tabooed marriage between members of a clan, and, for that very reason, unusual among Pulayar. Kiliyan was not willing to follow caste norms. He loved Kunjazhaki that much. So when he became an outcast in the community, Kiliyan joined the Holy Church, got baptized, and thus solved the problem.

Kiliyan acquired a new name—Pathros—and Kunjazhaki became Maria. There were others of Pathros's caste who also became new

Christians. The relief was that they were all allowed to build homes on the land around the Church.

All these stories flashed across Thevan Pulayan's mind. Kiliyan's old form passed through his memory like a streak of lightning. Things had changed so much since then. Today Pathros was one of the true believers of the Hilltop Church. He had greyed. A silvery string-like moustache grew thickly on his cheeks. He took the Gospel with him wherever he went, even to the field he worked on, reaping and threshing paddy. ... A great compulsion. As he stepped onto the embankment, he would take out the holy book from the woven bag and read one or two sentences. He would close his eyes and pray for a moment.

It was to the house of that true Christian that Thevan Pulayan and his son Kandankoran were going.

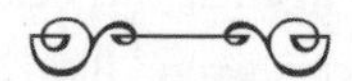

5
Asylum

The hill stood facing the fields, the horizon crimsoned by the onset of twilight. Lush young coconut trees, jackfruit trees with green leaves adorning their sprawling branches, and flourishing *moovandan* mango trees together created a verdant scene. The hillside was rendered beautiful in this manner. The rays of the setting sun hung like golden drops over the green fields. Old Thevan Pulayan and his son Kandankoran were climbing the steep path up the hill.

The day was coming to an end.

The Church stood on the crest of the hill, its beautifully sculpted cross embracing the infinite blue of the sky: a beautiful sight. The dying rays were painting the cross red. To look at it you would think that the drops of blood that splattered the wooden cross two thousand years ago had not dried yet.

Nam … *Nam* … *Nam* … The bells sounded repeatedly. There must be evening prayers in the Church. You could see the believers—men and women—climbing the slope through the many paths that led up to the Church.

Thevan Pulayan stopped. He was panting. There was a time when he could easily climb that hill to the very top, where the Church stood. Gone were those days. Now he had reached a stage where he had to stop at intervals if he wanted to climb the hill. He stood panting. '*Eda k'datha,* is there much further to go to reach Pathros's shack?'

'Just a little.'

Kandankoran pointed towards the tiny shack that stood behind the *muthira* fields, surrounded by four coconut trees. That was believer Pathros's home. Thevan had not been there for a very long time.

They stopped in front of Pathros's shack. Wild climbers entwined the fence made of thorny bamboo poles. Thevan Pulayan stood near the bamboo fence and looked around. The yard and the tiny house gleamed yellow in the twilight hour.

'Oh my, who is this? Who has come?' Maria stepped out of the house. The dark face brightened with a look of pure joy. She moved forward. 'Thevachayan and Kandankoran *k'dathan*. You finally remembered to come here after all, Thevachaya!'

They ducked as they stepped on to the veranda of the low-roofed shack. Maria looked inside and said, '*Edi*[1] Anna *kidathi*,[2] place a woven-leaf mat here.' She turned and said to the visitors, 'The girl is very shy.'

Anna *kidathi* appeared in the doorway like the rays of the sun at dawn. She spread a mat in the veranda and went inside immediately. She was not fair. Neither was she very dark. Her complexion was unusual, her youthful form was beautiful. As she disappeared behind the woven door, her slanting gaze shifted as it slid over Kandankoran.

Thevan sat down heavily on the mat. Maria asked conversationally, 'Achayan,[3] you'll want to chew some betel, won't you?'

'Mmh.' Thevan's face bore a look of utter dejection. The shadow of suppressed pain lay hard on that face with its greyed moustache.

Maria told her daughter, 'Anna *k'dathi*, fetch that betel box.'

An arm adorned with thin glass bangles extended through the doorway holding the betel-leaf box. Maria leaned forward and took

[1] A way of addressing someone (feminine). *Ediye* is also used sometimes.

[2] Girl or daughter. *K'dathi* is a variant of this term.

[3] Used with Christian names to show respect/affection (used within the community). C*hayan* and *chaya* are variants.

it, then placed it respectfully before Thevan Pulayan. He had a vigorous chew then spat into the yard. His head dipped once again as painful thoughts crawled across his mind like blood-sucking leeches.

'Where is Pathrochayan, Ammi?'[4] asked Kandankoran, trying to make conversation. They had come to these people's home, desperate for a place to stay; how could he not ask at least that? Was it right to sit silently?

There came Anna *kidathi*'s soft answer from inside. 'Achan has gone for a prayer meeting.'

Did honey drip from that voice? Though he heard it with his ears, he felt as though something sweet had fallen into his mouth. Forgetting himself Kandankoran stared at a gap in the woven wall. Like soft music that sinks into the soul's inner recesses, Anna *kidathi*'s voice echoed in his ear. Her voice seemed to resonate in the air.

Believer Pathros had gone to some house to pray. It might be very late when he returned. They would have to wait; there was no other way out, was there? Anna *kidathi* was busy in the kitchen, cooking. Shouldn't they give the visitors some food? She had been yearning to see Kandankorachayan for so long. Finally he had come, after she had borne the terrible agony of waiting and loneliness.

However, she was happy. When she was a young girl Kandankorachayan had been a frequent visitor. At that time he did not do any particular work. Now he had grown older. Responsibilities had increased. In spite of all that, he had come at an unusual hour, bringing his father along with him. She was relieved.

Kandankoran too was experiencing a certain strange feeling, as though he had swallowed something warm. He looked around him. He thought he could see two large, intense blue-black eyes through the gap in the woven palm-leaf wall. He stared back at them. Four eyes locked. A spark flared. A moment when a silent yet

[4] Shortened version of *ammayi*, meaning 'aunt'.

meaningful message was communicated; did he not experience a thrill at that moment?

After a while Maria spread a woven mat in the other corner of the veranda, near the kitchen. She brought water in a copper vessel and said politely, 'Achayan and son, come wash your hands.'

Thevan Pulayan got up quietly, his lips lengthening into a smile of sorts. He murmured, 'There was no need.'

Even when he rinsed his hands Thevan Pulayan continued to smile but the smile lacked life. The ache of suppressed pain made his face look wan. Kandankoran, too, rinsed his hands and sat down. Maria placed a clay pot full of rice in front of them.

Kandankoran sat with his head bent forward, eating. The old man asked questions occasionally, waited for the reply and smiled the same lifeless smile. Two dark wide blue-black eyes watched Kandankoran. Once in a while deep sighs fell on the thick silence and dissolved. In this manner, time slipped by.

They got up after the meal. Anna *kidathi* came and picked up the vessels.

Having rinsed his hands, Thevan wiped them on the clay-smeared towel that lay on his shoulder and leaned back on the mat. He pressed his head against the mud wall smeared and made firm by Maria with a mixture of coal and cow-dung. Utterly exhausted, Thevan closed his eyes. As for Kandankoran, he continued to stare at the eyes that watched him through the gap in the woven wall. He began to daydream.

'Is everything okay in the *thara, k'datha*?' Maria started talking to Kandankoran. He was eager to respond. Thereby, silence ceased for a while. From inside the room, behind the door, the soft musical sound of bangles could be heard from time to time.

Kandankoran said in a low voice, as though to himself, 'We no longer have a *thara*, Ammi.'

Maria looked at him, stunned. She could not believe what he had said. She asked, anxious and bewildered, 'What … what are you saying, *k'datha*?'

Like one swallowing bitter medicine, Kandankoran replied, 'Yes, Ammi. Tham'ran threw us out, me and Achan.'

From inside, Anna *kidathi* exclaimed: '*Ayyo, ente theivame*!'[5] She looked out, her face bewildered. Kandankoran's life had struck a hurdle. How could she watch him in that helpless state and not react?

Anna *kidathi* felt fear ignite within her. She wondered: '*Ayyo, ente theivame*, what is to be done now!'

For some unknown reason the glow on Maria's face faded. She was very fond of Kandankoran. She had known him from a very young age. In the dark handsome Kandankoran, Maria had seen her future son-in-law. But why should she send her daughter with a man who did not even own a shack?

Anna *kidathi* must have noticed the change in Maria's expression.

They sat wordless. No one had anything to say. An uncomfortable silence lay about them. The evening was drawing to an end. Darkness unfurled in the stillness of twilight.

It was really dark now. Anna *kidathi* lit a tin lamp and placed it in front of the door. The copper flame swayed gently. As he sat staring at the flame, Kandankoran's eyes grew moist.

The glimmer of a torch appeared near the barricade made of bamboo. Slowly the small light drew near. Thevan who sat leaning against the coal-and-cow-dung-smeared wall stood up. He rubbed his eyes and looked around.

'Is it Pathrochan?'

Pathros entered the yard holding a dully glowing torch. The next moment he raised the torch, making it burn brighter and looked at the veranda. He recognized the visitors. Pathros said joyfully, '*Deivathinu sthothram*, praise the Lord! Who is this who has come!'

Pathros was seeing Thevan after a long time. Their friendship was a rare and firm one. Time had not dulled it. A warm smile appeared on Pathros's face. 'I thought Thevachan had forgotten us all.'

[5] Unlike Thevan's exclamation of *ente paratheive*, this phrase reflects the influence of conversion to Christianity.

'How can one forget?' asked Thevan tiredly.

Pathros stooped and got onto the veranda. In the grave voice of a householder, he asked loudly, 'What did you give them, *kidathi*?'

'Served them rice, Acho.'

'Hmm,' Pathros grunted, satisfied. He then sat down beside Thevan and said with regret, 'I heard, Thevacha. That is the way of the world. We plan one thing. God allows something else to happen. We will have crosses and enemies. True Christians have to suffer all this.'

Pathros continued to talk. He was vocalising the belief system he had learnt from the Church. There is hardship and humiliation in this world. True Christians have to bear hundreds of trials, one after the other. A Christian's victory lays in bearing these trials bravely. Worldly life is transient. The lasting one is the life above, in the happy land of Canaan.

'Praise! Halleluiah!' Pathros exclaimed enthusiastically. '*Deivathinu sthothram*! Even if we have to suffer trials and hostility, we must live for God.'

Pathros got up from the mat and went into the kitchen. He asked in a low voice, 'Is there rice, Anna *kidathi*?'

'There is, Acho.'

Anna *kidathi* placed a bowl of water for her father. Pathros sat down to eat. Maria placed rice in front of her husband, no curry. She asked, 'Did the meeting end early?'

'Hmm.'

'Did the priest and preacher come?'

'*Hmm.*'

Silence once again. Pathros finished supper and got up. Maria got up too. That was an unusual occurrence. That wife had never behaved in that manner before. It was obvious she wanted to say something grave.

'May I say something?'

Pathros turned. 'What?'

'Kandankoran *k'dathan* and Achan, how long will they stay like this?'

'What is this?' There was displeasure in Pathros's voice.

'No, I was just saying. They don't have a shack, they don't have anything. They have left their *thara*. Where will they stay?'

Pathros made no reply. He just stood there, bowed head, thinking. What were the thoughts that wormed their way through that head?

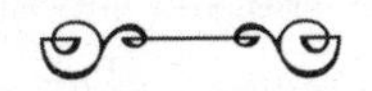

6

For a Spiritual Awakening

Non-believers Thevan and son began to live in true believer Pathros's home that stood on land belonging to the Hilltop Church. That was news indeed! The news spread like forest fire. Murmurs arose among the believers of the Church. Pathros had joined the Church and had baptismal water poured on his head. He was an enlightened member of the congregation. It was in that Christian's home that non-Christians Thevan Pulayan and son had come to live.

The Church stood on the very top of the hill. Towards the south, well into the shade of the spreading cashew-trees stood the Mission House, the bungalow where the parish priest lived. Sexton Mathai stood on the tastefully carpeted floor of that house. The silk curtains in the windows fluttered in the breeze. The sexton's eyes reflected a shade of suppressed anxiety. After waiting for some time, he called, 'Acho.'

'Who is it?' A question flowed out in a voice like the sound of a conch. It was the priest's voice, the plump parish priest who gulped from a chalice superior wine that came from Rome. The sexton, of course, recognized the excess fat for what it was. He moved nearer to the door with the swaying silk curtain that led to the priest's room.

'It's me—sexton.'

The priest came out. He wore a long white cassock that reached his ankles. The garment had a slit in front, from top to bottom, with thick buttons sewn over the slit. He was short and plump. Seeing the sexton, a broad smile appeared on his face.

'Why have you come so late in the evening, sexton?'

A watery smile appeared on the sexton's face. A smile that said, 'Nothing in particular; yet there is something all the same.' He said, 'Custodian Thomachettan said that he was coming here in the evening.'

The priest thought for a while. Custodian Thomas was an important person in that place and a member of a well known family, a family going back to the time Apostle Thomas came to Kerala all those years ago. People who knew history had many things to say about the family. All the older members of that family had been custodians of the Church in their time. The advantage of that circumstance was entirely for the Church! Custodian Thomas never hesitated to help God and God's men. He gave money freely.

It appeared he was coming to the Mission bungalow that evening! Custodian Thomas was not the kind of person who visited without sufficient reason. Not just that, he had sent sexton Mathai to inform the priest about it.

'Do you know why he is coming?'

'No, Acho.'

Achan walked up and down the room lost in thought. Some grievous problem that concerned the Hilltop Church must have come up. It could well be an issue that could rock the very foundation of their Church. Who knew what the matter was?

The priest continued to walk back and forth. After a while sexton Mathai said, 'Acho, sexton is leaving.' He stepped out into the yard.

Time passed. The evening light entered the big room of the Mission bungalow and filled it. The twilight rays that filled the room spread a bloody hue on the whitewashed walls. The priest stood for a while staring at the wall, at the picture of Jesus Christ hanging on a green wooden cross on Mount Calvary. He stared at the picture with anguish. Even the drops of blood dripping from Christ's body were painted on it. Was it the crimson of that blood that filled the room?

Jesus Christ had died for *chungakkarum papikalum*, tax collectors and sinners. For sinners … for human lives that had fallen apart, for those who were aching and sobbing with pain. The ones who had received libation from the holy blood would be saved! … The priest thought of those who had been saved in that manner. So many, many human souls! Pathros was one of them—Pathros, the devout believer from Pallithara!

'Pathros is such a good Christian!' the priest thought.

The dark form of that pious Christian emerged clearly in the priest's mind. The man lived in a low-roofed thatched shack on the southern side of the Church. He worked in the paddy fields and on the hill slopes. He harvested the fields, threshed and measured the grain. He tilled and turned up the soil on the hill slopes to grow tapioca. What a life it was! Bone-breaking labour! Yet, he was so content! None of the wealthy members of the Church knew how to pray the way Pathros did. His prayer had life because it took shape in his heart.

'Pathros really knows how to pray.'

The delicate silk curtains continued to swing gently. The day's light was fading. The servant lit a lantern. In the circle of light thrown by the lantern, the priest continued to walk back and forth. Soon he heard the sound of footsteps in the yard thickly laden with sand. Someone was walking up the yard. Who could it be?

The priest moved towards the door and peered into the darkness outside.

The visitor carried a lighted torch. The priest asked, 'Who is it? Is it the Custodian?'

'Yes, Acho.'

Custodian Thomas and two prominent members of the committee stepped onto the veranda together. The priest smiled. He sat down, settling himself firmly in the chair. The others followed. In the picture on the wall behind the priest's chair, Jesus's holy blood dripped, drop after drop …

'Sexton said you would come,' the priest initiated the conversation. 'Anything in particular?'

'Oh, nothing much,' Custodian Thomas laughed softly, respectfully. 'We must plan the meeting. It should be held at the end of the month.'

'Yes, we should do that,' agreed the committee members.

At the end of every month a special meeting was held in the Hilltop Church. On that day preachers from other parts of the land came and made inspiring speeches. This time, too, the end-of-the-month meeting had to be held, for which they had to find a good preacher. That responsibility rested with the committee members.

'We must invite a preacher who is truly spiritual,' one of the committee members observed. As he said this he raised his eyes upwards. He was remembering the event long long ago in Roman times when the Holy Spirit had descended on the apostles in flaming tongues as they had sat together in an upper-storey room in Jerusalem.

'Yes, that is a must. Expense does not matter. By God's grace the congregation of the Hilltop Church has the money to spend. But the preacher must be an inspiring one,' Custodian Thomas said.

The priest nodded and said, 'We will think about all that. So tell me, whom should we invite?'

Over the years several preachers had come to preach at the Hilltop Church. In some years there had been great awakenings, a time when each human soul had trembled under great pain and suffering. Filled with repentance, they had wept. Many men and women rose and bore witness to the Lord: 'I … I … am a terrible sinner. I … have hurt the Lord … a lot. From now on I will live for God.' Then they broke down, sobbing, racked by remorse.

The priest recalled all those stories. He hoped there would be a similar awakening this year as well, as had happened in the years '105 and '83.[1] At each of those meetings, awakening wrought by

[1] Years in the *Kolla varsham* (Malayalam calendar).

the Holy Spirit had increased. 'Oh Lord, if only there was a similar awakening this year!'

With this desire in mind the priest asked, 'Shall we send for Preacher Pathros?'

Custodian Thomas trembled when he heard that question. The committee members too sat dazed, unable to speak. What was it that they had heard? Invite Preacher Pathros? They all knew Preacher Pathros, they knew him very well. That was why they were shocked. Black as coal, hair that stood up like a bush, frail body, Preacher Pathros's face stood and smiled in front of their mind's eye. Skinny Pathros had a powerful throat. His words were loud and audible, like those heard through a mike. The preacher was adept in getting souls to repent. But … Preacher Pathros was a *puthu kristyani*! A new Christian!

They could not forget that. How could they? The thought made the Custodian and committee members shudder. Oh, why did Preacher Pathros have to be a newly-converted Christian!

No one said anything. The priest asked sharply, 'Why are you not saying anything, Custodian?'

Custodian Thomas looked at the committee members. He saw the answer on each face but no one said anything.

'Tell me. Shall I invite him?' asked the priest, in a hurry to arrive at a decision.

'Thing is … Acho, you should not misunderstand,' Custodian Thomas began, embarrassed, his voice cracking. 'We don't want Preacher Pathros.'

'Yes.' The committee members agreed. 'We too don't want Preacher Pathros to be called.'

'Why?'

'Well, he … isn't he a new Christian?'

The words pierced the priest's heart. Had Custodian Thomas, who had been born in an ancient family, evolved only so much? Could he not listen to a new Christian—one they had freely admitted to their religion—preach the Gospel? Was that to be seen as demeaning?

Stroking his beard the priest observed thoughtfully, 'Preacher Pathros speaks eloquently. That is the important point.'

They all knew about the preacher's extraordinary powers. That voice was enough for waves of repentance to surge in the congregation of the Hilltop Church. It was equally possible that the glow of the Holy Spirit might kindle a spark of life in that congregation. That was good too, no doubt about it. The congregation's spiritual light might burn brighter thereafter.

For the priest the important thing was not who the preacher was; there should be a spiritual awakening in the congregation. He had been waiting for it for so long. He said sharply, 'We have to make a decision.'

'We must,' Custodian Thomas became engrossed in deep thought. Creases appeared on his broad forehead, drops of sweat too. Images of long dead and one-with-the-earth forefathers of his ancient family flitted across his mind. His family had existed from the time Apostle St Thomas had landed on the Kerala coast. It was an ancient family. Its beginning could be traced to one of the ancient Brahmin families. Though he was a believer of the Christian religion, he was not willing to give up his elite status. Unconsciously the thought arose in his mind, 'Am I so trivial? My family has existed since the time of Apostle Thomas. Oh God, those times!'

Custodian Thomas felt his head starting to ache. Seemingly intolerable thoughts swarmed his mind. The heat was unbearable. He broke out in a sweat. Thomas wanted to go out, to feel the cool breeze. It was impossible otherwise. Blind pride was squeezing that man's soul. *Ho!* What suffocation is this!

He felt as though his ancestors had risen from their graves, assumed hideous forms and were standing hidden by the dark. Custodian Thomas trembled. He looked out through the open window. The world had gradually sunk into darkness. Against that dark background the forms of his ancestors seemed to grow huge, like mountains. The forms were becoming clearer. They said in one voice, 'Please do not bring a Pulaya preacher to speak in the Church!' The words gained echoes like the thick sounds flowing out of a cave.

Were these just fanciful thoughts?

Custodian Thomas stood on the veranda of the priest's bungalow, bathed in sweat. He could not arrive at a decision. Just then two hairy hands fell on his shoulder. Startled, he turned his head and looked through the corner of his eyes. The priest stood right behind him.

Achen asked gently, 'Why did you go out without taking a decision, Custodian?'

Exhausted, Custodian Thomas re-entered the room. He sat in a chair and leaned back. The committee members were thinking hard. One of them said, 'I am willing to have Preacher Pathros invited.' He smiled broadly and said, 'Whichever preacher comes, I and my wife will come for the meeting and proclaim witness.'

The priest's face brightened. 'That is the important thing,' he said.

So, it was decided! Custodian Thomas's head sank forward. There could not be a greater humiliation than this. In a split second all his grandeur had crumbled. Like thick sounds echoing from a cave, the voices of his bygone ancestors sounded pleading yet frightening: 'Don't do it!' It was like a roar. Did no one else hear it? Custodian Thomas looked around him. Was he the only one, did no one else hear it?

He had to rescue the prestige that was about to disintegrate. He had to make one last attempt. He looked piteously at his fellow committee members, a look that pierced the heart, that said many things.

Custodian Thomas said tactfully, 'Acho, all you want is an effective speaker, isn't that so?'

The priest nodded, 'Yes.'

Custodian Thomas continued, 'If you bring Preacher Pathros half the people will be displeased. So we'll do one thing. We will invite another equally effective preacher.'

That was indeed a suggestion. The committee members nodded in agreement. The Hilltop Church had been established by foreign missionaries a hundred years ago. Then it was that for the first time in Kerala, one who belonged to a low caste had been baptized. There were many people in the Hilltop Church who had been converted from the low castes. The new Christians formed about half the congregation. They would indeed be happy to have Preacher Pathros speak to them. But it was Custodian Thomas who was at the helm of the congregation. A decision that he did not approve could not survive there. As a prominent member of that congregation, as a representative of the upper castes, he should prove that clout, shouldn't he?

After thinking deeply Custodian Thomas said, 'We'll invite Preacher Stephen.'

The committee members nodded their consent. The priest, too, had nothing against it. Stephen was a good man. He belonged to the upper caste. Even if his interpretation of the Gospel was not inspiring, it was not bad. Custodian Thomas and his friends need not hear a 'Pelayan preacher' speak, after all. The Lord had saved them. The Lord was so merciful! As for the new Christians, they did not have an opinion in such matters. Even if they had, they would not say it. Who were they anyway? They were just listeners, weren't they? What else could they be?

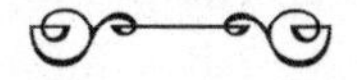

7
Preacher Stephen Arrives

The fair plump Preacher Stephen arrived, accompanied by five people. One of them was his assistant, whose job it was to repeat every sentence he said during the sermon. The remaining four were singers. A few musical instruments and a large bundle made up their luggage.

Buses plied on the public road that circled the bottom of the hill. The preacher and his group had boarded the 4.30 bus. By the time the bus reached the junction where three roads met beneath the Hilltop Church, it was past 6 o'clock. The bus stopped the minute the conductor said, '*Stap*, please!' The preacher and the others got down with some difficulty. The bus began to move immediately, stirring up dust that rose into the air before swirling and settling again. The preacher pulled out a handkerchief from the pocket of his loose tunic and covered his nose. Once the dust settled he looked around him, wide-eyed. Hadn't anyone come to welcome him and escort him to the Church?

Just then he saw Custodian Thomas approaching him with folded palms, smiling. He began to talk almost immediately, 'Welcome, Preacher. We will go to the bungalow.'

In the tone of a philosopher, Preacher Stephen said, 'It's getting dark, is it not?'

The Custodian nodded in agreement.

'Is it very far?'

'*Aayee*, no. There, that's the place.' Custodian Thomas pointed upwards. The Church stood proudly on top of the hill that lay drenched in the yellow light of the sun. The rays fondly stroked the cross on its top. Indeed, it was a sight that stirred the heart! Preacher Stephen gazed at the sky above the cross that glowed in the light of the setting sun. He said in a low voice, '*Sthotram*, praise!'

Custodian Thomas walked towards the tea-stall nearby saying, 'Quick, serve us four–five teas.'

The stall-owner moved towards the jug. Custodian Thomas dusted a bench and called: 'Preacher, just sit for a while before we go.'

The preacher and his troupe entered the shop in a single file and sat down on the bench. Custodian Thomas told the owner, 'Quickly please, Pillaicha.'

His forehead smeared with sandalwood paste, Pillaichan mixed tea-dust, sugar and milk. He poured the tea into glasses with a whirring sound and stirred each briskly with a *tik tik* of the spoon. He then placed the glasses in front of the men. Watching the steam rise from the glass the preacher smiled. A bland smile. The shrewd tea-stall owner asked, 'Anything to eat, Thoma *mapp'le*?'[1]

'What do you have in your almirah, Pillaicha?'

Pillaichan opened the wooden door at the back of the glass-framed cupboard wide—*parippuvada, boli, bonda, ethakkaporichathu*, a variety of savouries. The preacher and his fellow travellers had their fill. The tea-stall owner must have made a substantial sum.

They stepped outside. The distance to the Hilltop Church was hardly five furlongs. If you went up straight it was just three furlongs. But that path was not safe. Even if it was a bit of a roundabout way, it was better to go along the longer path. Preachers, of course, would never take the twisted path!

But, there, too, they faced a difficulty. The singers had brought their instruments and a big bundle. How were they to get these to the priest's bungalow? Custodian Thomas looked at the verandas of the shops that lined the junction where the roads met. A

[1] Vocative form of *mappla*, the term used in central Kerala to address Christians.

dark-skinned boy, his body covered with sores, sat scratching his back. Custodian Thomas asked, '*Da*, can you get these to the bungalow?'

'Oh, ready.' The boy twisted a skimpy worn towel into a ring and placed it on his head like a crown. He balanced the instruments and the bundle on his head. A really heavy load! The poor boy almost bent double under the weight of the instruments meant to add sweetness to the hymns rendered up to the Lord. He walked ahead. Preacher Stephen, his group, and Custodian Thomas followed.

'This is the preacher who has come to speak at our Church meeting,' Custodian Thomas told Pillaichan as he departed.

When they were out of hearing, Pillaichan said: 'That lot of preachers! They preach and get the poor Parayan[2] and Pulayan to join the Church. What for? To exploit and exclude them.'

Hearing this, other customers in the tea-stall chuckled. Kali Parayan sat crouched in the corner of a bench gulping down black coffee. He had come to sell a woven-leaf mat in the evening market. Hearing Pillaichan's words he grinned bitterly, showing teeth stained from chewing betel.

'That is the truth, Koch'amra.[3] Why do they make us join the Church? To enslave us.' He stopped to gulp down the rest of his coffee. Replacing the glass he said, 'But that's not it, Koch'amra. We, too, have our gods and deities. Then how can we join the Church?'

The people in the tea-stall laughed, but Kali Parayan could not. He looked sad. It was as though painful thoughts filled the old Parayan's mind. It must hurt him to see people of his caste converting to Christianity. The old Parayan repeated to himself, 'We, too, have our gods and deities.'

Where were the gods and deities? Were they asleep on their stone platforms in the corners of yards? Were they not watching

[2] Parayar is another untouchable caste. The members of this caste carried the tag 'Parayar'.

[3] Young lord or master.

their people sacrificing their beliefs, changing their names, and joining another religion?

Kali Parayan sat, head bowed, upset.

Pillaichan asked, 'What are you thinking about so deeply, Kali Parayan'e?'

'Oh, it's nothing, my Tham'ra.'

At this time a welcome ceremony was underway in the Mission bungalow of the Hilltop Church congregation. The minute he saw Preacher Stephen, the priest came out and shook his hand. The next moment the preacher raised his loose tunic-covered arms and embraced the priest. It seemed as though two festive waves were embracing each other. Laughter resounded in the air. Conversation began like water gushing out when the shutters of a dam are lifted.

Preacher Stephen asked, 'The meeting starts today itself, doesn't it?'

'Yes,' the priest nodded, 'One week—till next Sunday.'

The Custodian had a suggestion: 'Let us announce the meeting on Sunday night as the time for people to bear witness.'

The Preacher had nothing against the suggestion.

Preacher Stephen was quite old. Even when he was a teacher in the school owned by the Mission, he used to preach in the church nearby. He had the skill to do both jobs with ease. The local folk knew him in both capacities; Christians called him 'Preacher', while non-Christians called him 'Sir'. As for Stephen, he responded to both with a smile.

Between preaching, teaching, and listening to the call of the Lord, Preacher Stephen had grown really old. Time wrought many changes. His hair greyed, his face and skin wrinkled, and however much he tried to resist it, he developed a stoop. At the age of sixty when he retired from teaching, he became restive. How could he sit around doing nothing? He was not used to it. People had stopped calling him 'sir'. One morning the preacher walked into the nearby tailor's shop. He stood before the tailor with a roll of white cloth and said gruffly, 'Listen, I need you to make a loose garment for me, very loose.' Fixing his spectacles on the tip of his nose, the preacher sat down, leaning firmly. The tailor was bewildered. Why? What for? He had tailored for the preacher several times. If you saw those shirts, you would think they were meant for young men. You would think the preacher had not realized that time had staked its claim on him. He was that great a stickler for fashion. Yet, here he was; as the needle of the sewing machine flew forward, the tailor wondered: 'Why … why the change?'

In the next few days everything became clear. People saw the preacher standing at the corner of the street wearing the loose garment, holding a black leather-bound Bible edged with red. Preacher Stephen cried out, 'Sinners, come to me! The kingdom of the Lord is open to you!'

From that day onwards Stephen began to preach, holding his black leather-bound Bible, its pages tipped with red. The result was amazing. He preached the message in many places.

It was certain that there would be an awakening, now that he was here.

Preacher Stephen asked with a clipped smile, 'What is the spiritual state of the congregation?'

'There is some kind of dullness.' The priest sounded frustrated and grief-stricken.

The preacher raised his voice, 'How else can it be, when Satan is running around like a roaring lion, looking for a victim to fell! Christ's brides must stay awake and pray. Or they will fall into temptation.'

Custodian Thomas said, 'The word of the Lord is true. The Holy Book says that Satan is out like a roaring lion looking for prey. We all know who that is.' His words were heavy with innuendo.

Preacher and priest looked at the Custodian. The singers who had accompanied the preacher were sitting in the next room, tuning their *tampuru*. The cymbal produced an enchanting sound.

The Custodian continued, 'Satan, the roaring lion. Do you know who that is, preacher?'

'Who?'

'Communism. It is about Communism that the Lord speaks in the Bible. We, the true Christians, should be extremely vigilant.'

Everyone fell silent. The priest was thinking about what the Custodian had said. It was indeed a serious problem. The problem had been discussed in the Hilltop Church before this. A large number of the new Christian members of the Church lived in an area called Kochumolumbram. The locals had given the place another name, Moscow. Most of the new Christians in that area had communist sympathies. It was said that the arch communist Ramakrishna Pillai visited the place at night! Many had seen him in Pillaichan's tea-stall at night!

Custodian Thomas said with a conspiratorial smile, 'Preacher, there is something you simply must do. When you speak you must mention the danger. It needs to be told to the new Christians.'

The Custodian continued to talk. He had grave matters to discuss. The new Christians were forming a union of agricultural labourers. They were becoming its members. They knew many things they had not known before. They asked questions boldly. Class sense had awakened in them. When they hear that they have been exploited for centuries, when they realize that the fruits of their labour were enjoyed by rich farmers and land owners, won't they be furious? The instinct to resist is innate. It cannot be stopped. These days something else has entered the heads of those new Christians. When he thought of that, Custodian Thomas grew really nervous. They had recognized the upper-caste dominance in the Church. The true Christian Pallithara Pathros had asked, 'Did you make us join the Church to make us slaves?' In the storm raised by that question the foundation of the Hilltop Church was shaking.

Preacher Stephen's gospel-preaching was to begin at a time when the unpleasant atmosphere was beginning to eat into the Hilltop Church.

8
Temptation

That evening the bells of the Hilltop Church began to ring. That was unusual. Pallitharayil Pathros was engaged in serious conversation with Thevan. The visitors had to be served the night meal. In ordinary circumstances it was enough to chop up the fleshy leaves or stalk of something that grew in the yard, sprinkle some chilli powder, and make a curry. But today that would not do. Anna *kidathi* took a spade and went to the southern side. There was *kannan* colocasia growing there. She dug around two or three clumps, pulling out big pieces of yam along with the rich, dark, fertile soil around them.

Maria called out, 'Anna *kidathi'ye*, bring it quickly, will you?'

'Oh, here, here.' Anna *kidathi* wiped off the mud around the tubers, gathered them into her basket, and hastened towards the house. There she picked up the sickle and began to scrape off the skin. Maria came to the veranda just then. Pathros saw her face peering through the gap in the woven doorway. He stopped talking and walked up to her.

'What is it, *edi*?'

'Come here.' Maria led her husband towards the back. She asked gravely, 'Is it enough to sit like this?'

Hearing the accusation Pathros's face became sombre. He bowed his head. The woman of the house was accusing the householder. When two visitors come to the house, the man of the house should not sit idle, ignoring household matters. That was wrong. Pathros acknowledged this when he asked gruffly, 'What is it, *edi*? Tell me what it is.'

Maria said: 'Our Thevachayan and *k'dathan* have come, haven't they? I'm asking out of ignorance; don't we have to serve them rice and curry?'

Again Pathros's face paled. To make food for two grown men was an expense in a Pulaya shack. Maria hinted as much. Pathros replied loudly, as though angry, 'What kind of talk is this!'

There was harshness in that voice. It was not the kind of talk that happened between a husband and wife whose hearts beat as one. It was as if they were blaming each other. They were not willing to support each other, to lend each other a hand in their hour of need. Anna *kidathi* heard the conversation as she sat scraping the colocasia pieces. She was frightened. If the visitors seated on the woven mat in the veranda overheard any of this! It would be such a shame!

Maria realized she had been too blunt. She was only happy to have visitors. She was ever willing to serve them food. But was that enough? You could serve rice and curry only according to what you had. Pathros was not responsible either. Maria said, 'Why are you scolding me? I just said something, that's all.'

Pathros, too, was regretting his outburst. He said, 'What did you say? You said nothing.' Looking searchingly at his wife's face, he asked, 'Isn't there anything for the night meal, *edi*?'

'There's rice and I made gruel, but …' Maria asked in a low voice, 'Curry has to be made, isn't that so? I need a coconut.'

She pointed towards the coconut tree that stood in the yard and said: 'If you can pluck a coconut or even a tender one.'

'What are you saying, *edi*? No, I won't do it.' Pathros refused. He would continue to refuse. He could not do it. The coconut tree was on Mission property. Authority to pluck coconuts was vested with the Church. True believer Pathros was only a tenant and did not have the right.

Maria was annoyed. 'Then what will I serve the guests?'

That was true. Pathros looked at the coconut tree, his thoughts weighing down on his soul. The coconuts hung in thick bunches.

It was Pathros' hands that had planted the saplings in the Mission soil. But when the trees grew and bore fruit, the Church people came and plucked all the coconuts. Pathros just looked on. All these years the Church men had come and plucked the coconuts, and Pathros had looked on. He had no complaints. He did not even think that they were denying him his right. Complaints arise only when there is awareness, isn't that so? Anyway, Pathros refused to pluck coconuts from the Church's coconut tree. That poor soul believed that it would enrage the Lord.

Maria stood nearby, her face swollen with anger and discontent.

True believer Pathros looked at the tree, at the bunches of fruit. It was a terrible moment of temptation. He shut his eyes tight and held his breath. Lord, he prayed, let me not succumb to this temptation. When he opened his eyes his gaze was again on the tree trunk, bathed in the fading light. That true believer was being tempted. In the beginning, in the beautiful scenic Garden of Eden, Satan came in the form of a serpent to tempt the grandmother of all mankind—Eve—Pathros recalled. That image would not go away, it haunted him. Perhaps that was the reason Pathros felt that the long slender tree trunk was the snake's body. His eyes jutted, frightened. The same intense desire that shone in Eve's eyes shone in the eyes of that poor man. Yes, yes ... it was exactly the same way. The coconut tree stood in front of him, tall, swaying. The yard of that Mission hut with its tapioca, pumpkin creeper, and plantain was transforming into the Garden of Eden. The bunches of coconuts were like the enchanting fruit in the Garden of Eden. The angry woman beside him, her head tilted to one side, her sad eyes filled with teardrops that looked like bits of glass; she was like Eve. He was like the deeply tempted Adam. Oh was he turning into vapour? He could not think. He made up his mind. Pathros folded his *mundu* and tied it. He caught the trunk and began to climb. *Dum dum dum* ... coconuts began to fall.

Maria cried, '*Ayyo, ente thaivame*, enough.'

Pathros climbed down the tree. His face was flushed. Beads of sweat gleamed on the tip of his nose. Something was pushing against his chest, as though he had eaten something forbidden. He felt he was a sinner. To commit a sin knowingly; what a terrible thing that is! Pathros walked towards the veranda with bowed head. As for Maria, she picked up the coconuts and went inside to her daughter.

At that time the bell was heard again from the Hilltop Church. 'What is that Pathrocha, the sound of bells that we hear?' Thevan asked.

'It's the Gospel meeting in our Church; it starts today!' Pathros felt tremendously proud when he said it. He was proud of the spiritual progress of his Church. It was evident in those words.

The ringing of the bells spread down to the twilight blues of the valley.

In the homes of the new Christians the night meal was just being prepared. The men and women had been working in the paddy fields all day, the dark-skinned women bending down, plucking the saplings and sowing them separately. Simultaneously, they threw bundles of saplings towards the male workers who caught them and took them to sow farther away near the outer ridge. Work stopped only at six. The women then went to Mundakkamoola pond and entered the water to bathe. They pounded their clay smeared *mundu* against the nearby rock before washing them. The men, meanwhile, went by way of the Village Development Centre and bought cheap sack-rice, *beedis*, and card-mark matches from Kavungottathu Varkey's shop. By the time they reached their shacks and the rice was on the stove, night had fallen. The gruel was yet to be poured into bowls.

* * *

Old Outha Pulayan said, '*K'datha*, there's a meeting today.'

Paulos asked, 'Who is the preacher?'

Outha Pulayan said, 'Who else? Preacher Pathros, of course.' A picture of the preacher with his coal-black skin and thick frizzy hair flashed in Outha Pulayan's memory. 'It's really great to hear Preacher Pathros.' That night he would hear the dear preacher speak. Outha Pulayan felt excited as he thought about it.

However, fair plump Preacher Stephen had come to preach to the Hilltop Church congregation. But did poor Outha Pulayan or that true believer Pallithara Pathros know about it? Those new Christians were getting ready to go for the meeting. At that moment, alone in his room in the Mission bungalow, Preacher Stephen must have been leaning against the door and praying to the Lord Almighty. Would there be a spiritual dawn?

It was not yet completely dark. The western sky was even now suffused with a crimson hue, like the blush on the cheek of a young woman. However, the majesty of the night was growing.

From the open windows of the Mission Church, the glow of the lantern shone.

Sexton Mathai went to the bungalow. The priest, Preacher Stephen, and the group of singers were already seated at the big table in the dining room. They were having a meal with many dishes. Seeing the sexton the priest called out, 'You're here, sexton! Ring the second bell.' He drank some water and continued, 'Check if everything is ready, the mats, benches, whatever. Then come and have supper.'

'*Mmh.*' Murmuring assent, the sexton walked towards the Church. In the pure light emanating from the open door, the sexton's form could be seen moving forward. A long shadow followed him like Satan following the believer.

The bell sounded again. Waves of sound spread over the workers' homes built all around the Church. Pallithara Pathros and family heard it. Pathros said, 'The second bell has also rung.' He stood near the visitors watching them eat, still burdened by the sense of guilt. He had done that which was forbidden. His heart was aflame like a stove. He had no peace. That poor man had done something that would not find favour with God. Pathros recalled the prayer they said when they admitted their sins on Sunday,

We did what we should not have done.
Neither are we content.
Even then, O Christ, have mercy on wretched sinners like us!

Pathros felt his guilt ease and peace fill his heart when he said the prayer in his mind. His face brightened.

He said, 'I need to go to the meeting.' Pathros looked at Thevan's face as though seeking permission.

Thevan said, 'Then go for the meeting Pathrocha. I would like to sleep.'

Mental exhaustion had worn out Thevan Pulayan. Maria turned towards the house and said, 'Anna *kidathi*, fetch a mat and spread it for Achayan.'

Anna *kidathi* came out into the veranda and spread a mat. She placed a pillow as well. There was no scarcity of mats in a Kuttanadan Pulayan's house. Every woman was an expert weaver. The broad ridges that bordered the fields were lined with *pula* palms bearing thorny crowns. Women would cut the sheaves, bind them and carry them home on their heads. They would sit in the shade of the coconut trees, legs outstretched, and cut the sheaves. They would remove the sharp needle-like edges. Only then could they fold the sheaves. Bundles of sheaves kept to dry could be found on the shelves of every Pulaya shack. Once the rainy season set in, women had no work. There was no harvest, no sowing of saplings. At that time women would unfold the sheaves, rub and clean them carefully, tear them into fine pieces, and weave mats. While doing this they would sing in voices oh so melodious!

As for the pillows in Pulaya homes, they were unique. There were no sewn pillow covers made of beautiful cotton cloth in those shacks. Instead, there were woven pillows filled with hay. These were not soft, but one's head rested comfortably!

Maria said, 'Spread a mat for Kandankoran *k'dathan* next to it.'

A light glowed in Anna *kidathi*'s liquid eyes. There was a new brightness across her cheek bones. Even in the dark of the night, the beauty in her expression was visible. She moved forward, her black bangles giggling sweetly. She spread another mat. A strange ache took shape in her heart. She herself did not know the reason for it. When she went back into the room, a hitherto unknown feeling brimmed in her heart.

'Then I will go to the meeting ...'

Pathros walked towards the Church.

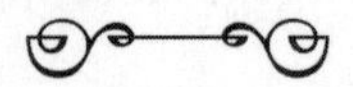

9

Look at the Birds of the Air …

The Church filled with people long before the meeting began. The new Christians in front, behind them the ones with ancient Christian lineages. In that group there was Custodian Thomas, who could claim a glorious family history which dated back to the time Apostle Thomas came to Kerala. At the back of the Church there were benches with backrests. The upper-caste Christians heard the true Gospel leaning back against these comfortably. That was a must. They had the 'licence' to sit in that manner. At the time of celebrating Christ's last supper, they would get up from these benches and kneel before the *maduvaha*.[1] Once they received the holy Eucharist, they would return to sit down again and relax.

However, right in front, woven mats were laid for the low-caste Christians. Their fate was to sit on the floor. But they had no complaints about it. That was because they had never considered this a grievance at all. For them, even to sit cross-legged on the floor in front of those upper castes was a privilege.

From among the 'believer' women rose a song of praise:

There is no fairer
Bridegroom than he …

Like a curiosity of the month of Kanni, young girls sat in rows, singing Gospel songs in the light of the lantern. Nice rhythm, melodious music. Those virgins yearned to sing about the fair and rose-hued divine bridegroom, the one who stood out as the

[1] Malayalam equivalent for mizbeach, meaning altar.

noblest among ten thousand men. They sang; creating a dream-like world ... feeling that the bridegroom was standing just in front ... rapturous; the young women felt their hair stand on end. The rhythm gained speed—with cymbals, drum beats and jingling bells. Even the soulless Christian songs—when they flow from the throats of Pulaya women, made melodious by singing '*tithana-thithanna*', while plucking and replanting paddy saplings—throb with a newly-gained inner life!

The Syrian Christian women sat at the back watching it all. The bright rays of the lantern kissed their heavily-powdered cheeks.

The meeting was about to begin.

The priest walked up to the table. The song ceased. Absolute calm descended on the scene.

'Beloved children of Christ, the meeting is about to begin. By the grace of God, we have been sent a good servant of the Lord to bring about a spiritual dawn, and to enable God to touch and awaken our hearts. Praise be to God!'

Everyone—true believer Pallithara Pathros, old Outha Pulayan and Paulos—waited for the preacher to appear. Their eyes were directed at the door. They sat expecting to see Preacher Pathros enter, with his coal-black skin, thick black hair, and lean body, pressing the Holy Bible to his chest. Minutes—one, two, three—crawled by. Why was the preacher, whom they awaited with eyes wide open, not coming? Would he come only after exhausting their patience?

Custodian Thomas leaned back against the back-rest firmly, his face grave.

The dim glow of a lantern could be seen moving from the Mission bungalow towards the Church. It was sexton Mathai holding the lantern. Just behind him walked the well-fed Preacher Stephen. Pallithara Pathros, Outha Pulayan and Paulos watched them approach the doorway.

Pallithara Pathros asked in a hushed voice, 'Who is that coming to the Church?'

Old Outha Pulayan's eyesight was weak. He said to Paulos, '*Eda* Pauloth'e, just look and tell us, young Pelayan'e.'

Paulos quietly opened one of the shutters of the window and looked out, screwing up his eyes. A light-skinned preacher, stout, short. Seeing the preacher in the flickering light of the lantern that sexton Mathai held, Paulos lowered himself and said in a defeated tone, 'That is not our Preacher Pathros.'

Outha Pulayan was shocked. So was Pallithara Pathros. Pathros was a member of the committee. In the eleven-member committee, nine members were Syrian Christians and two were new Christians. Pallithara Pathros and Outha Pulayan were those two new Christian members of the committee. The committee had decided to call Preacher Pathros for this year's meeting. Preacher Pathros, with his coal-black skin, thick black hair and lean body; and now …

The light flickering outside stopped at the doorway, its coppery hue magnificent against the pitch dark outside.

The priest was saying, 'Preacher Stephen, whom God has sent to preach the holy word to us this year, has arrived.'

At that moment Preacher Stephen followed the sexton into the Church. People's faces brightened with respect. The preacher walked straight to the table, knelt on the woven grass mat spread there and prayed for a long while. He was about to preach. Therefore, he must pray devoutly for God's mercy. The Syrian Christians said to one another in hushed whispers, 'Preacher Stephen's speech is really *pasht* class, first class.'

Pallithara Pathros felt as though his heart had stopped. He stared like an idiot. That poor man could not understand it at all. What was his reaction? As a member of the committee, he was being humiliated for the first time in his life. Pathros was proud of being a member of the congregation of the Hilltop Church and of being a member of the committee. That pride had suffered a beating. He felt ashamed, angry. Why not call Achan, ask what had happened. He had to find out. But he was not smooth-tongued and was, therefore, helpless.

Preacher Stephen's group of singers began to sing melodiously.

Old Outha Pulayan whispered into Pallithara Pathros's ear, 'A different preacher is here!'

Pathros, who continued to stare, nodded, still dazed. Even at that time, a picture stood out in his mind of a man with coal-black skin, a lean body, and thick black hair. It was a distinct picture. The long thin arm held a leather-bound Bible edged with red. He looked at the true Christians and spoke passionately. Such an enlightening transformation it was! Unknowingly Pathros' eyes filled with tears; they poured down his cheeks ... warm tears dripped on to his lean chest.

Preacher Stephen's fervent speech was gaining in intensity. The assistant's repetition echoed louder.

'Look at the birds of the air,' said the preacher. 'They do not sow, or reap, or store away in barns. Yet, your heavenly father feeds them all. Then ye of little faith, are you not much more ...?'

The speech went on and on in this manner. This world was a myth. There was humiliation and hardship in this world. In the world above there was no humiliation, no hardship. It was heaven. Men of little faith begin to fear and despair when difficulties appear. When you reign in the heavenly Canaan with Christ for thousands of years, all difficulties will end. That day Christ will wipe the tears of his pious virtuous brides.

Preacher Stephen roared. His voice rose, his body broke out in sweat, streams of which poured down the wrinkled folds of his neck. The preacher within the preacher awoke. What vitality! What a clear voice! The intensely passionate speech went on, negating all physical reality in the process.

Pointing his finger at the people, Preacher Stephen proclaimed: 'And therefore, Christ is weighing your souls.' The assistant raised his voice to repeat: 'And therefore ...'

Custodian Thomas and the priest were greatly impressed by the sermon. Pallithara Pathros, too, sat mesmerized in that whirlpool of sounds. He was a low creature, eternally sorrowful, one who could not claim anything as his own in this world. Some bits and parts of the speech went straight to his heart. He awoke. There were things for him to remember.

'So do not worry saying, "What shall we eat?" or "What shall we drink?" or "What shall we wear?", for the Gentiles eagerly seek all these things.'

Under Preacher Stephen's skilful eloquence, the sigh that lay heavily in the corner of Pathros's soul disappeared. Wasn't that speech a representation of his life? Pallithara Pathros swelled a bit. His sunken eyes grew moist. In this wide world he was eternally experiencing sorrow and meanness. There was no one to lament for him. When the time came, when he reigned in heaven with the angels for a thousand years, Christ would wipe away his tears. Like the bridegroom who holds his virgin bride close to his chest, Christ will embrace him. At that time his dark-skinned body would be transformed into a rose-tinted one. He sat smiling as though he actually saw the transformation and the heavenly Canaan in his mind.

The preacher's two-and-a-half-hour long speech came to an end. The audience sat motionless. No one could even move. Custodian Thomas and the parish priest felt an intense satisfaction as though they had drunk heavenly nectar. Preachers should select passages like these when they speak. So relevant!

Custodian Thomas ran his eyes over the women seated on the other side. Tears of repentance ran down every cheek. They were regretting their actions, repenting. Good, the parish priest thought. Let them regret and repent. Let their selfish sinful hearts be washed and cleansed by those tears of regret.

The parish priest got up and came towards the table: 'Dear ones of Christ, today's meeting will end with the prayer of repentance, which will now follow. If God permits, the holy meeting for spiritual well-being will be held here tomorrow as well.' The moment he stopped speaking, drops of sweat appeared all of a sudden on his forehead. He took out his handkerchief from the open pocket of his cassock, whereupon a slim shining chain which held together a bunch of keys fell out. It fell to the floor with a tinkling sound. The preacher leaned forward to pick up the spread-out bunch of keys and pressed them into the priest's palm. The keys belonged to locks that kept secure not just the priest's personal wealth, but also that of the Church and the *maduvaha*. The priest pressed his handkerchief firmly against his sweat-covered forehead and wiped it. He said, 'There is something important I want to tell you. It's about the offering to be made to our preacher. By God's mercy he has come to our midst with the Gospel. Praise be to God's invaluable mercy! But the servant of God has a family and children. As Christians we have the duty to take care of the family of the servant of God. Therefore, from tomorrow we will have the holy thanksgiving contributions along with the meeting.'

He sat down. Again the beautiful lyrics of a song arose from where the dark women sat in rows. Those women were born to sing. How they sang! The entire symphony of heavenly music must lie in their throats. That was why they sang. They sang even in the paddy fields. That musical inheritance flowed into the Church as well, that was all.

The song ended. There was a prayer at the end of the meeting. The message of each day's sermon would transform into that prayer. That was how it was routinely done. Custodian Thomas meditated and prayed over the message God the Lord had delivered through Preacher Stephen on that first night of the meeting. He wept. Finally, that crowd of men and women knelt down and prayed, murmuring like bees in a hive:

'Amen!'

Hundreds of dots of light set off from the Church on top of the hill—lanterns, torches, and lighted palm shoots. The lights scattered into the illusion- and desire-ridden valley. The crowd dispersed.

Custodian Thomas asked in a whisper, 'Acho, how was the speech?'

'It was very good,' the priest replied, nodding approval.

The low-caste Christians left as a group. Pallithara Pathros held a lighted torch of palm sheaves high in his right hand. Right behind him was Outha Pulayan. Behind him Paulos. Heated thoughts filled the minds of those poor men, rushing into their hearts—thoughts that they could not articulate.

Paulos was the youngster in the group. He asked, 'Why didn't they call our Preacher Pathros? Why bring an unknown preacher from somewhere?'

That was indeed a question. A question that pierced the heart like a chisel. Even Paulos, who had asked the question, might not have realized it would be so sharp.

Outha Pulayan replied, 'Who cares who the preacher is? Wasn't it an effective speech?'

Pallithara Pathros had no doubts regarding that matter. He nodded vigorously.

'That is true.'

Paulos, however, had an even harsher question to ask. It was this: 'No, I'm asking out of ignorance. Both of you are in the committee, aren't you? You said Preacher Pathros would come. And we came to hear him speak. Finally, who made the speech?'

Pathros made no reply. Old Outha Pulayan, too, could not reply. Once again, certain heated thoughts forced their way into their hearts. They continued to walk silently, heads bowed.

10
Outha Pulayan's Warning

The meetings continued to take place in the days that followed. People from other congregations, even men and women from other sects, came in large numbers to the Hilltop Church. What an exhilarating coming together! Custodian Thomas had not thought the meeting would be such a success. Neither had the parish priest. The meeting had created a real stir. The priest could not contain his joy. Was not the apathy that had for some time enmeshed the congregation disappearing? Was not a spiritual rebirth happening? He stood watching the people crowding the Church ... it was just like a valley in flower!

The new Christians participated in everything wholeheartedly. At first some of them felt resentful that one of their own had not been brought to preach. However, perhaps it was a trait that was in their blood—the inclination to question grew cold and died.

Pathros said with amazement: 'What a speech, that preacher's!'

He himself went around to every house to collect the offering of a fistful of rice. It was actually sexton Mathai's responsibility, but he was a lazy fellow. Sexton Mathai was not really interested in all this.

Thus, Pathros reached the elderly committee member Outha Pulayan's home. It must have been past four o'clock in the evening. Outha Pulayan's home was built on the edge of a cluster of fields that lay long and vast, going on and on. When Pathros reached the house Outha Pulayan was sitting on a woven mat in the shade of a coconut tree, weaving a basket with the rib of the coconut leaf.

It was meant to catch fish when water flowed through the sluice into the field.

'Pathroth'e, come here,' Outha Pulayan called invitingly. When he came up the old man asked, 'You seem to be in a hurry. Why?'

'Oh, nothing. I came to ask for your contribution of a fistful of rice.' Pathros replied.

That was what Outha Pulayan did not understand. What right did Pathros have to ask for the fistful of rice? It was sexton Mathai's responsibility. He was the sexton of the Church. Why should Pathros come with the rice bag hanging from the crook of his arm?

Pathros had not expected such a question to be flung at his face. He felt tired. He stood for a moment, as though thinking, then said, 'Isn't a speech being made at our Church now? To have the preacher staying in the bungalow is a huge expense. So Achan asked me to come and I came.'

Outha Pulayan accepted the explanation. However, there was not a single grain of rice in that house. No smoke had risen from the roof that morning. Terrible want. It was that time of year when the watering and plying of the wheel was done, when the leaves of the paddy plant begin to slump as grain begins to fill each stalk. Now the Kuttanadan Pulayan had just one job to do—to guard the paddy. There was no payment for that job. Guarding the crop was the Pulayan's responsibility.

Now he had to wait for harvest season. At that time a silver coin will clink into the Pulayan's tobacco basket. New grain would fill his *puttil*, the woven bag used to store paddy. Many more days had to go by before that time dawned. Till then, water was drawn in the homes to cook gruel depending on what time it was. Right now a spider had spun its web around the edge of the mud pot.

The thought of not giving to the Church did not even occur to Outha Pulayan. As a committee man it was a matter of honour to contribute his share without fail—the one-tenth, the fistful of rice and the first crop. It needed to be given correctly and completely. Or else people would mock him. Not just that, if he contributed to

God's work, the greater would be God's blessing. Outha Pulayan asked, his voice breaking: 'What should I do?'

Pathros was in the same situation. There was not a grain of rice or paddy to be had from his house either. But as he was a tenant of the Mission-owned land, he had the good fortune of being able to grow some ten shoots of tapioca and make a meal of it. That was a big relief. Besides, there was his wife, Maria, and daughter, Anna *kidathi*, in his house. Anna *kidathi* was one of the ablest among the young women who went to harvest in that land. Maria, too, was equally good. True, she could no longer harvest like before. She had grown old; her back would not bend like it once did. Truth to tell, Pathros had married Maria … he unconsciously recalled that story. They had stood in the same row, moving forward as they harvested the crop. It was evening when Maria straightened her back. She was still holding the sickle. Pathros could harvest only eighty bundles. And Maria? One hundred and fifty! She stood with the lovely bundles of thickly laden paddy shoots lying in a row behind her—a beautiful sight!

So in Pathros's home there would be fresh paddy even after the harvest was over. Rice gruel could be had at least once a day in that house. Outha Pulayan had no children. He and his wife lived alone, with no one to help. In his youth he had had two wives. One of them went off with Kunjolu Velathan, who came to beat the drum. It was said that they had built their home on the south-western side of Chambakkulam, somewhere in Thakazhi! At harvest time Outha Pulayan would enter the field with a *puttil* in his arm-pit, and follow the women who stood and harvested in a row. Sitting and crawling, he would pluck the few paddy shoots that had escaped the sickle, bring them home, and separate grain and chaff. He would then sieve the grain and measure it. He would tie it up in the *puttil* and place it on the shelf above the stove. That was over. What would he do now?

All that was true; but he could not withhold the portion he needed to give to the Church, could he? If he died they would not permit his burial in the cemetery. Outha Pulayan had a son by the wife who had deserted him. He had been an infant sucking at his mother's breast when she left. The boy lived with his mother. He might call Kunjolu Velathan 'Acho', but would that satisfy him? Even today that son's heart must be thirsting to call Outha Pulayan 'Acho'. He would surely return, wouldn't he? When he came, he too should be made to join the Hilltop Church. For that to happen, Outha Pulayan should not be a debtor of the Church.

Pathros said, 'Outhachayan, you must give the fistful of rice every month.'

'That has to be done,' Outha Pulayan nodded. Helplessness shadowed those sunken eyes. The shattered desires of a lifetime could be seen in them. Outha Pulayan said, 'I will always stand by the Church.' His voice shook.

From the time he had joined the Church, Outha Pulayan had lived like a true Christian. Drinking, drum-beating, performing black magic, it had all come to an end. He had never walked that path again. He obeyed the parish priest and Custodian Thomas, and would continue to do so. But who would remember all these merits when one became a debtor?

Pathros asked, 'Shall I go then, Outhachaya?'

'*Hmh*.' Outha Pulayan lowered his head, and began to tear out the thin needle-like rib from the tip of the coconut leaf. Pathros began to walk, holding the rice bag in the crook of his arm. He took four steps forward, then stopped to look back. Scratching his greying head Outha Pulayan had called him back.

'Come here.'

'What is it?' asked Pathros. 'Is there a way out, Outhachaya?'

Poor Pathros thought he had been called back for the fistful of rice. Perhaps Outha Pulayan had found a way out.

'What is this that I hear?' asked Outha Pulayan gravely, dropping his voice.

Pathros stood clueless, bewilderment spreading across his face. He asked, stammering, 'What is it? What is it Outhachaya?'

Outha Pulayan took out tobacco from the folds of his *mundu* and began to chew it. His mouth full of juice, he continued, 'You're a young Peleyan. You do not see the possibilities of what could happen in the future. That's how it is, I was saying.'

Outha Pulayan continued: 'All these are serious matters. There are certain rules to be followed by the Parayan and Pulayan who join the true religion. That set of rules keeps his life tightly bound. They are not something anyone can break. Even if one had the strength to do it, one should not. Religion forbids it. He became a new being when he became a Christian. That was what the parish priest had taught them. No one can do anything against it. The chains of organized religion were that strong. Therefore, we must live as Achan tells us. That's how it is.'

After a pause Outha Pulayan continued about the life of a true Christian believer. Outha Pulayan was repeating it the thousandth time. What pleasure could there be in hearing that which one had heard so often that the ear had become desensitized to it? But Outha Pulayan was not saying it for pleasure. One must obey the parish priest, the committee and the Custodian. He had not thought beyond that. Practice, too, should follow. Beating the drum, killing roosters, doing black magic, making offerings in temples—all these were taboo for the new Christian.

Pathros heard it all. With courage freshly gained, he asked, 'Why are you saying all this to me, Outhachaya? Which of these did I do?'

'Eh lad, Pathroth'e, I'll tell you. I don't mind telling.' Once again he chewed and, in the zest of chewing, he scratched his head. Pathros suddenly felt a flash of fear, as though something had ignited within him. He was going to hear something ominous. What was it? Maybe some time, without his knowledge, his wife or daughter had done some black magic. Outha Pulayan was talking as though he knew all about it.

'What is it, Outhachaya? Tell me, whatever it is.' Pathros' heart was beating fast. But however much he thought, he could not imagine his wife or daughter performing *velathan kottu*.[1] Maria would never do it. She hated it. In the evening when Pathros said the prayer, she came and knelt by his side. She would weep at that time. How could such a one perform *velathan kottu*?

'I'll tell you lad; Pathroth'e I'll tell you. Who do you think has come to stay in your home?'

'What do you mean "who"? Our Thevachayan and son.'

'Ah. That is what I said. I, too, know Thevan. He has his gods and deities. He calls on Melathan. Can you have him stay in your house, boy?'

The naked truth had come out in its true form. What he had done was wrong. The error was a grievous one. Pathros wondered why he had not thought of it earlier. He had erred, particularly when he was a tenant of the Mission Church. He should be more loyal than other members of the Church. Where others folded their hands, he must lie face down in supplication. Without doing so he could not live. If the parish priest or the Custodian harboured a grievance against him, it would be terrible! He would have to tear down his house from the Mission-owned land. Shouldn't he be careful?

That tenant who did not have land of his own should always fear the owner of the land.

However, he lived on Mission land, and not on the land of any individual landlord. He was not the slave of any landlord. He worked independently for his livelihood. He went to work for whoever called him. In the evening he would claim his wage of two measures of paddy, tie it up at the corner of the thin towel that he placed on his shoulder and return home. He worked on the Mission's property as well. Sometimes he worked for Custodian Thomas who had land behind the Mission Church on the northern side, where a hundred banana trees could be planted. This time the *onthekadan* variety of

[1] Velathans are a sub sect of the Pulaya caste who perform caste rituals, use cowry shells to predict auspicious timings, and engage in ritualistic drumming. *Kottu* is the ritual beating of the ceremonial drum.

tapioca had been sowed. The previous year it was the large plantain. Pathros had gone to till and dig up the land around the tapioca crop, and to build the boundary wall. But he was not the servant of any landlord. However, in spite of all that, Pallithara Pathros had to be careful. He did not have a title deed; he had no land to claim as his own. Complete power over the Mission property was vested in the parish priest.

Outha Pulayan chastized him in the tone of an experienced elder. '*Eda* lad, Pathroth'e … therefore, you should send Thevan and his son away. That is what you should do.'

The joy Pathros had felt that morning waned. His enthusiasm died. It was as though his heart had suffered a pounding. He began to walk or rather, his feet walked without his knowledge, along the ridge by the paddy field. Far away, behind the island lined with young coconut trees, he could see the hill top, covered with green, interspersed with homes and yards. On its forehead stood the Church. To see it stand like a white lotus was indeed a magnificent sight. Just behind the Church on the southern side stood his home. He could not see it. That tiny house must be hidden among the lush green growth all around.

Pathros stood there watching for some time. What might be the thoughts crossing his mind? A Hindu and his son were living in his house. It seemed like Custodian Thomas had not heard the news till now. Or he would have told the parish priest. Achan would have called Pathros to the bungalow; removing his thick framed shining spectacles and placing it on the cloth-covered table, he would begin to rebuke him. Nothing like that had happened. Pathros thought he was a coward. He was hurting himself by imagining things that had not happened. When he thought about it he almost laughed. Nothing like that had happened. Pathros began to walk.

What Outha Pulayan had said was a just warning.

There were many more homes that he had to visit, the homes of the rich Christian landlords. He had to go to those homes; his rice bag would fill only if he went to those houses. Moreover, they might feel pity on seeing his exhaustion and give him something to eat. The remains of the previous night's supper or a burnt dosa … something. Whatever it was, they would give it to him instead of mixing it into the mush fed to the cow. That was what he should remember. … Pathros quickened his pace.

11
In the Name of the Living God

The Gospel meeting was to end that day. The crowd was so thick that if one threw a fistful of sand, not a grain of it would reach the ground. The parish priest's joy was great indeed. Custodian Thomas strutted about with the air of a hero. Who had arranged for such a triumphant ending? Doubtless, the Custodian—no one else. The congregation was indeed lucky to have such a good Custodian!

The tent was teeming with people even before nine o'clock. The song of the dark-skinned women rose and filled the air. The upper-caste women sat silently at the back in a row of benches, wearing expensive clothes, their necks, ears, and fingers shining with ornaments. The nightingales were singing. So also the black cuckoos. What business did the peahens have there?

They imagined that sitting silently without singing added to their consequence. The subconscious attempt of the human mind not to admit defeat!

Grey-haired and stout, Preacher Stephen stood up to bid farewell—was it not, after all, a sweet pain? The preacher's voice broke. The devout men and women watching, wept.

'Look at the birds of the air.' The preacher repeated this and several other phrases. The people were not bored by the repetition. The preacher continued to speak. Finally, 'So do not worry, saying, "What shall we eat?", "What shall we wear?", "What shall we drink?",' he concluded. Then he sat down.

Absolute silence spread over the gathering. Now followed the golden opportunity to bear witness. The dark-skinned Christians stood up quickly one after another, bore witness and sat down.

At one point they must have thought themselves to be the birds of the sky. Was that not indeed the truth?

Yes, that was the truth. Those innocent souls had nothing to claim as their own in this wide world. They did not have granaries. They did not store anything either. Their entire life was a long and painful struggle with no one sympathizing with them. But they did have one comfort. Men and women in the community worked shoulder to shoulder and consoled one another.

In all sincerity Pathros felt that the saviour Jesus Christ had had him and his people in mind, when he had narrated that story so beautifully. He sat with closed eyes, praying. That poor Pulaya Christian also thought, 'God Almighty is to be praised.'

The meeting ended. Pathros returned home. He moved the woven screen from the doorway and stooped to enter the house. Maria was not yet asleep. He lay beside her and whispered in her ear, 'The meeting is over, *edi*.'

To hear him one would think he had returned after performing some great deed. Maria replied listlessly, 'Is it? That's good.'

Pathros found her casual, indifferent reply intolerable. He said with the authority of a husband, 'What, *edi*, you speak so lightly of it?'

'What "lightly"? You said the meeting was over. So what should I do?'

Pathros had so much to say about that meeting! It filled his heart to the brim, waiting to splash on to the tip of his tongue. He wanted mainly to talk about the speeches he had heard. Oh, if only she had heard them! She cursed Pathros when there was no rice in the house to cook gruel, or for not paying their dues in the shop. Oh, she knew nothing about the word of the Lord. Nothing! Or else would she not know the holy words from the Gospel, 'Man shall not live by bread alone but by every word that comes from the mouth of God.'

He had so much to talk about. Pathros continued to talk. Maria merely grunted in reply. His rough voice rumbled *patha para* like rain drizzling on the old woven roof, but she was not convinced by any of it. She said the upper-class preachers merely say all this. Pathros was shocked. Look at the evil of ignorance! He said earnestly as though taking an oath, '*Edi*, in the name of our living God, all this is written in the book.'

Once again Pathros had uttered an oath in the name of the living God. That new Christian had learnt to say it that way. The Bible said Jehovah alone was the living God. The other gods and goddesses were just stones and blocks of wood! That was why Pathros despised Anjilthara Thevan Pulayan and his son, Kandankoran, who worshipped a piece of granite as their deity, *karumadikuttan*, sacrificed roosters, and cut the stem of the banana tree and threw it as part of their ritual, performed pooja and recited mantras. It was hatred born of religious teaching! He had to oppose the Hindu Pulayar though they were his people and his relatives. He could not contain that hostility churning within.

In order to make Maria understand better, Pathros said with emphasis, '*Ediye*, it is written in our Book. And it is the truth. So don't behave in a mean or greedy manner. You must not say such things either. You think only about eating and drinking.' He again quoted the line. Maria lay quietly for some time. Maybe she was thinking about eating and drinking. For that uncivilized woman, for that poor Maria—who had worked in the clay-filled field and the grassy hill slopes from childhood onwards, and was now exhausted—was it possible to think of anything else? Had she not lost the ability to think clearly?

'Is there anything for tomorrow, rice or tapioca, anything?'

Pathros had the duty to answer that question. He had a duty to do so. It would be dawn in two or three hours. The sun would rise from behind the row of hills in the east. Pathros, Maria, daughter Anna *kidathi*, they all had to go for work. How could they go without eating anything in the morning? For that, something should be cooked in the house. They had visitors too. Thevan Pulayan had come with his son, empty-handed. Not to serve them food would be against Pulaya tradition.

The Pulayar were the race that nourished other folk. At one time, long ago, they had been the owners of the land. At that time there had been rulers among them. But the ones who came as beggars double-crossed the lords and, over a period of time, turned them into slaves to work for them. Today, the Pulayar did not have a grain of soil to call their own. Yet, they were happy. They drew water and drenched the fields and grew paddy. The plants flourished and hung, loaded with grain. The very sight of it filled the Pulayan's stomach. Even if he had to go hungry and suffer hardship, he would never abandon a guest.

'Let's forget about us. We won't eat. But what will we give Thevachayan and son?' asked Maria.

'*Deivam Thamb'rane*!' Pathros lamented, a long, heart-rending cry. Did God Almighty hear that cry? Pathros, who grew paddy and gathered it into mountain-like heaps, lamented with an aching heart the lack of rice to cook a meal. There were tears in that lament. At that moment he remembered Preacher Stephen who had told them not to think of what to eat and what to drink. Maybe it was true for the preacher. Pathros had seen him at the dining table in the parish priest's bungalow. What a lunch the preacher received! Pathros's mouth watered remembering it. Oh, when he thought of it, poor Pathros felt, 'All that the preacher said were lies!'

Intense anger welled within him. Words and interpretations to scare the poor! He cursed his own stupidity for believing it. Almost immediately, he repented. Whatever it may be, he was a true Christian! Was it right for him to think in that manner?

However, Pallithara Pathros could not refrain from thinking about food. Perhaps the true Christian within him was dying inch by inch. Or else, because of the intense nature of his painful experiences, he must be making new decisions. That was indeed a change. Could anyone deny it?

Pathros clenched his teeth and growled to himself, 'The birds of the sky … the birds of the sky …'

Thinking about it he fell asleep. At dawn Pathros woke up hearing the cry of millions of birds as they flew across the sky, flapping their wings and cooing sweetly. The sky had lightened. Yellow sunshine spread across the yard.

Pathros walked out into the yard rubbing his eyes. He saw Custodian Thomas before him. Pathros asked respectfully: 'What could be the reason for your presence?'

'Oh, just like that, but there is something.' Thomas moved towards the shade of the spreading coconut tree in the yard. 'Pathros, I came to see you. Come, let us walk farther down.'

They climbed down into the lane and walked forward, towards the sand-covered southern yard of the Church. They stood at the corner, bordering the cemetery. So many human lives that had sunk into the silent sleep of death! The mounds of sand that marked the burial ground of those poor souls were slowly flattening out. In the land thus laid bare, new burial pits were dug, new mounds of sand appeared. The sandy mounds were the graves of new Christians and poverty-stricken Syrian Christians. Those graves would erode over a period of time. The world would not remember that the Hilltop Church had such inheritors at one time because there were no memorials for them.

Then there were others—wealthy ones like Custodian Thomas, men with paddy fields that yielded a thousand measures of grain, who owned lakhs of acres of land, mansions and rubber estates. They too would die one day. Once they breathed their last, they too would be confined to coffins and taken to the graveyard. But their passing would be observed with pomp. A band would walk ahead playing soulful music. Waves of that music would fill the air. The local people would hear it. A sea of tearful people would move towards the cemetery, singing the dirge. If you see it, you would think that they had come as a deputation to God almighty to plead for the dead man. When a rich man died even his death became an event. People would gather in large numbers. There would be memorials for them, structures made of granite topped with white marble. Engraved on the shining white stone would be black letters that read 'Resting in God'.

To rest in God!

That practice had a flaw though; after a few years the mounds that marked the poor men's burial ground would erode and disappear. The rich mausoleums, labelled 'Resting in God', would stand with stiff necks amidst the emptiness. As years went by the marble mausoleums alone would mark the ancestors who had established the Hilltop Church and nourished its growth. Who would remember Pallithara Pathros after his time? But everyone would remember Custodian Thomas. Even in the cold frozen graves of death there was inequality between the rich and the poor.

Pallithara Pathros and Custodian Thomas stood at the corner next to the cemetery. Custodian Thomas asked meaningfully, 'Pathros Pelen is a committee member. You know that, don't you? ... No, I am just asking.'

Pathros did not speak. He understood that Custodian Thomas had dropped the bait to catch his prey. Pathros stood with bowed head.

The Custodian continued, 'When we are the Lord's congregation there are certain rules to follow. Pathros Pelen is a new Christian. So you do not know these things. You must not go against rules, particularly as a member of the committee!'

That was a serious accusation. A new Christian was ignorant, he lacked understanding! That was what the landlords thought. The Pulayar go to both church and temple. They have no basic understanding of anything. Did their lives have a definite goal? Was it wrong if the landlords thought in that manner?

But in turn Pathros Pulayan too could ask certain questions. The words throbbed at the tip of his tongue. Custodian Thomas talked about traditions and rules. No need to talk about traditions. Pathros knew all about them. From the outside his life might seem ineffectual and without meaning, but it still followed the Church's age-old traditions. There was no change in that.

Pathros could shut Custodian Thomas's mouth. An intensely powerful question took root in his mind. Do the rules of the Holy Church apply only to new Christians? Those with ancient lineages, those who talk of family grandeur dating back to the time Apostle Thomas came to Kerala, are they not subject to those rules? The committee of the Church had decided to invite Preacher Pathros to speak—Pathros with his coal black skin, lean body and thick hair. Due to just one person, Custodian Thomas, it did not happen. Not just that, Thomas brought another preacher called Stephen. Pathros was a committee member. He did not know about it. If he threw such a question in his face, Custodian Thomas would be stunned into silence. But Pallithara Pathros did not ask. Pathros was one who had buried in his throat many such questions that needed to be asked. His people, too, did not ask. Was it because the questions lacked strength? Was it because the questions would have no effect? Perhaps his children might dare to ask. Let at least the coming generation learn to question!

Custodian Thomas asked gravely, 'Who has come to stay in your house, Pathros Pelen'e?'

Pathros had to answer that question. 'One of our clan.'

'What is his name?' Custodian asked with a smile.

'Thevachan. His son is also there. His name is Kandankoran.'

Once again the Custodian leaked a twisted smile. Then he broke out laughing as though he had discovered a crime.

'*Eda* Pathros Pelen'e, can a committee member do this? On whose land are you staying?'

Pathros's nerves began to throb. Hot blood pumped into them. He stayed on Mission-owned land, land bought by the white missionaries for the poor Christians of the land to inhabit. They had done so out of piety when they saw the oppression the Pulayar had to face in the name of caste. The Syrian Christians latched onto the missionaries and tried to gain the upper hand. And now, questioning him! Should that not be resisted?

Pathros retorted, 'Whose land? Not on *your* land!' The words had the sharpness of a chisel.

Can he not ask at least that much? He, too, was a man, wasn't he? Custodian Thomas, who was not willing to accept him as a human being, trembled with fury. What did Pathros say?

'You have grown that much, have you, Pelen'e!' roared Thomas. 'I will put an end to your audacity. You will not allow me to deal with you kindly! You cannot live on Mission land and have a Hindu in your home. Isn't that what I said in plain language?'

Pathros watched Custodian Thomas as he pounded off angrily and entered the priest's bungalow.

12
Heartbreak

Pathros had done no wrong. He had not even thought of doing anything against the Church. But the parish priest and Custodian Thomas declared him guilty. Pathros had done something unacceptable, something that a true Christian should never have done. The news spread all around the Hilltop Church. Those who heard it made it their business to repeat it to others.

It was that time when both wheel and boat were being used to water the paddy fields on the southern side. Thevan Pulayan and son continued to stay in Pallithara like cows tied to a post. In between, Kandankoran found work for two days—breaking rocks in the quarry in Chovattu hill. It was Peeli who hired him.

There were other workers there, breaking rocks, who were not pleased when Peeli called Kandankoran. They chided Peeli, saying what he had done was unnecessary. When Kandankoran learnt this he refused the wages Peeli offered. He did not want anyone's pity. He was healthy and strong, and was one who worked for a living.

It was difficult to make ends meet at Pallithara. The days somehow dragged on, with or without any food. Maria cut grass, tied it into a bundle, and carried it on her head to the evening market to sell. She would get four or five *annas*[1] with which she had to manage the household. The paddy stored in the *puttil* on the shelf was over. Now if they wanted gruel they would have to buy rice.

Thevan regretted having put Pathros in such difficult circumstances. The old Pulayan was not used to it. He had never even dreamt that

[1] A coin of a certain denomination.

such a tragedy would befall him in the twilight of his life. But it had happened. Kandankoran too felt uncomfortable about it.

Thevan Pulayan spent every minute in fear. At any moment, Maria might say something harsh. He did not know when the word would fall from her mouth. It could happen at any time. Words were like live coal. The fire would spread quickly. The burns would be terrible.

Then, one day, a woman from a house nearby came to Pallithara. She wanted a *nazhi* rice. She would return it at harvest time. There was not a grain of rice in the shack. All Maria had to do was say that. But that which had been simmering inside her for many days came out thus: 'What can I say, how can there be rice or anything else? It's a curse! Our job is to feed visitors forever, isn't that so?'

Thevan Pulayan, seated on the other side, heard it. He shut his ears tight. He could not hear more. Were they words or embers of coal? They seared his body and soul. He burned in slow excruciating pain. Thevan Pulayan stared at life with eyes filled with despair. Gloom spread everywhere ... Not even a tiny ray of light anywhere. If there was any way out, the old Pulayan would have called his son and walked across that doorstep.

In the evening Pathros came burdened with sorrow. His head was bowed. He came and sat on the verandah, let out a slow sigh, and said, 'It's all pointless. Achan has sent a notice.' Pathros took out a paper from the folds of his *mundu*. What was written in it? What had happened, that the priest should write with such urgency!

Ignorant and bewildered, old Thevan Pulayan asked, 'What? What happened?'

At that moment two dark blue eyes stared out from behind the woven screen door. Anna *kidathi*, who had heard what Pathros had said, got up from beside the stove and came to the door. Her large dark blue eyes looked troubled. What was going to happen?

Old Outha Pulayan came tottering towards Pallithara. Anna *kidathi* said, 'Look, the *appan* from the other *thara* has come.'

Outha Pulayan walked with difficulty, his back bent double. It must be something serious that had made the old man rush here. As he reached the yard, Pathros rose respectfully.

'Outhachaya, there was no need to walk all this distance. I would have come there.'

'Will I not come if it is necessary?' Outha Pulayan said gravely as he entered the veranda. He sat down, legs outstretched. The words had the sharpness of a whip. Pathros shivered as though struck. The circumstance that had brought about Outha Pulayan's hurried arrival echoed in his words. That he could not walk added gravity to the situation. Obvious displeasure coloured his words. Outha Pulayan said, 'Achan sent a letter. I did not hear it read. I thought I will come here. Who will you get to read it?'

There was no one in the old man's shack who could read the handwritten note. His son Azhakan lived with his mother in Thakazhi. When she left he had been just five years old. Twenty-two years had gone by. Azhakan grew up in Kunjolu Velathan's guardianship, (the same Kunjolu Velathan who was now living in Anjilthara). If Azhakan had come they could have got him to read the notice. They would know what it was about. What a stifling situation this was! He wanted to know the contents. He would get no peace till he knew what they were. The poor souls sat holding the notices they had received, like monkeys holding unhusked coconuts.

That wait! What lay hidden in that tiny bit of paper? Would the message that lay hidden in those clear black letters be frightening? Pathros shivered, seized by an unreasonable fear. If only he had learned to read. He would not have had to wait interminably like this! The need for education had never struck him so hard before. But had the Pulayar deliberately decided not to study? No! Society—controlled by a set of norms that the upper castes had created in the name of God—would not permit it. Those norms were like iron, they could not be challenged or overcome. Even the government schools did not admit the children of Pathros and his like. The government granted permission and encouraged the education of low castes. But the heads of schools, blinded by caste norms, would not permit it. If Pulayan and Parayan entered their portals, those dwellings of Saraswathi would be polluted.[2] So they were refused admission citing one reason or another.[3] The seats are full. Go to another school, they would say. There were prophets of culture among those who said this. Because of all this, Pallithara Pathros and Outha Pulayan could not go to school. In spite of this, Pathros could read a little—a few familiar words in the Bible and the tracts printed in the Mission-owned press—but that was all. For the first time he felt the frustration of being deprived of education. What a loss! Thevan Pulayan said, 'When our Kandankoran comes, he will read.'

Pathros nodded as though agreeing to it, but Outha Pulayan was displeased by the suggestion. His son Azhakan should marry Anna *kidathi*. That was the old man's desire. Anna *kidathi* had beauty and youth. Her husband will be a lucky man. Not just that; if that happened, Azhakan would not live in Velathan Kunjol's shack anymore. The searing pain that Outha Pulayan felt in his chest whenever he thought of his son—that would end. However, Azhakan could not marry Anna *kidathi* as long as he remained Azhakan. But there was a way out for that. Azhakan should be baptized and made a member of the Church. If he became a new Christian he could marry Anna *kidathi*, a new Christian's daughter.

Outha Pulayan had many such dreams. Thevan's stay in that house might prevent his hopes from becoming a reality. Kandankoran was

[2] Certain Harijan children had been granted admission in Pullat Government School, south of Thiruvalla and Kunnanthanam (Maraman), and C.M.S. Mission School. That night the school was burnt down.

[3] Paul Chirakkarode's original note: A book published recently says: 'Isn't it enough that a carpenter's son remains a carpenter and an iron smith's son remains an iron smith?'

also handsome. Any girl might fall in love with Kandankoran, with his ink-black skin and muscular frame. Moreover, it was possible that Kandankoran, too, would get baptized and join the Church. Thevan might agree to it. They did not have a place of their own. In such miserable circumstances they might do anything! New Christians who did not have a home were allowed to build one on Mission land. Who knew, perhaps Anna *kidathi* might already be in love with Kandankoran.

Outha Pulayan said resentfully, 'I think it is about you allowing a young man to stay in your house.' He elaborated on the gravity of that folly. Anna *kidathi* who stood quietly behind the woven screen heard it. A lightning-like thought flashed through her heart. In its momentary gleam she saw everything clearly. So that is how things are, is it? She directed a question to herself. Is that so? Is it so? She loved Kandankoran—that was true. It was a bonding of hearts, there was no blemish in it. What was there for people to talk about so much? If a young man and a young woman stayed in the same shack, spent the night in the same shack, it was enough to set people talking. Sighing deeply, Anna *kidathi* thought: 'Let them talk their fill!'

They all waited. Someone will come. He will be a divine person who knows how to read. They would give the notice to that stranger. They would have no peace till they heard it read. When would that one come? As they all waited Kandankoran arrived. Forgetting her surroundings Anna *kidathi* said, her face alight with joy, 'Kandankorachayan has come.'

A grave look covered Outha Pulayan's face. Pathros understood it. Ignorant of it all, Kandankoran entered the yard. He stood looking at the immobile people for a moment. Anna *kidathi* stared at him, her eyes filled with worry. In a voice filled with anxiety Kandankoran asked, 'Why is everyone so quiet?'

The grave look on Outha Pulayan's face deepened. As she saw it Anna *kidathi* felt a pang of fear. She knew the reason for it too. He wanted Azhakan, his son by the wife who had left him, to marry her, to fasten the *minnu*[4] around her neck; that is what the old man wanted. It was not going to happen. A warm sigh escaped her. Her wide eyes slid over Kandankoran's strong ink-black body. No, only he will tie the *minnu* at the back of her neck.

Pathros said, 'Kandankoran *k'datha*, the Achan in the Church has sent a notice. Both of us have got it—me and Outhachayan. Take this *k'datha*, just read it, will you?'

Kandankoran took it and read it aloud. No one understood anything. Silence reigned. Outha Pulyan said, 'Read it once again, young Pelen'e.'

Kandankoran read it again: 'On ... date, Thursday evening, the committee will hold a meeting in the Church. Therefore, as committee member, you should be present during the meeting. Certain serious problems need to be discussed and decisions must be made in the name of the Lord.'

Thevan sat apart like an uninvited guest, not joining in the conversation. Kandankoran too did not say anything. What did those low-caste Hindus have to say in matters of the Church? *Poochakkundo ponnurukkunadathu karyam*?[5]

Among the new Christian members of the Church on top of the hill, Pathros and Outha Pulayan were the leaders, all set for the moment they would fly off to heaven. They had been called to attend a meeting of the Church committee, of which they were members. Neither Kandankoran nor Thevan Pulayan should voice their opinions on that matter.

It filled Thevan Pulayan with frustration that he had to seek shelter in the home of that new Christian.

Outha Pulayan, who had been lost in thought, roused himself and said to Pathros, 'What day is today, Tuesday, isn't it? So Thursday is day after tomorrow. Yes, day after tomorrow evening we will know.'

[4] The thin flat piece of gold with a cross engraved on it which is tied around the Christian bride's neck during the wedding ceremony.

[5] Malayalam saying meaning 'What role for a cat where gold is melted!'

Would they be able to remain at peace till then? He felt there was a lump of glowing charcoal in his heart. Without lightening his grave look, Outha Pulayan said, 'Then I'll take leave,' and stepped out. And thus the day ended.

The next day Pathros went to Pillaichan's teashop at the foot of the hill. He wanted a black coffee. He went to the separate shed-like veranda at the back, meant for the low castes. Custodian Thomas was in the tea-stall at that time, leaning back against the bench next to Pillaichan. When he saw Pathros his face darkened in anger. Blowing on the glass held to his lips Custodian Thomas said, 'Listen, Pillaicha, we Syrian Christians made a mistake. We are the old Christians aren't we? The ones with ancestry. We baptized some Parayar and Pulayar, sprinkled holy water on their foreheads, drew the sign of the Cross, and made them Christians. Do you know what happened in the end?'

Tea-stall owner Pillaichan wiped the sweat from his sandalwood paste-smeared forehead and asked, 'What happened, Thoma *mapp'le*?'

Pillaichan was always attentive to whatever Custodian Thomas had to say. It did not mean that he enjoyed the conversation. It was just that Thomas was the rich man of the region. On many occasions he had helped Pillaichan generously.

The Custodian straightened his back and continued. 'What happened, you ask? *Ente* Pillaicha, what more can happen? Parayan and Pulayan were allowed to join the Church. We, the early Christians, did not like it. But the missionaries insisted on it.'

Pillaichan knew that story was true. He did not have any great knowledge of history, but he remembered the story about the celebration that took place in the Hilltop Church some years ago. There were drums and yodelling, flag-hoisting and fireworks. A meeting had taken place at that time. Pillaichan remembered that a huge crowd had gathered at the Church. What was special about that day? They were celebrating the centenary of the day a missionary sahib had baptized a Pulayan and made him a member of the Holy Church. He remembered that many people had made speeches on that day. He asked, 'So what, Thoma *mapp'le*?'

'Oh, they are communists. They have no respect for the landlords. They think they can oppose us!'

Pallithara Pathros sat as if he had not heard a word. There were other Pulayar sitting on the narrow verandah at the back of the tea-stall. Kali Parayan entered just then, bamboo baskets on his head, one above the other. A grin leaked onto his face, showing rotten betel-stained teeth. He asked, 'What is it?'

Pathros went out without bothering to answer the question. Pillaichan called out from behind, 'You have not paid, Pathros Pelen'e.'

Without turning to look Pathros replied loudly, 'Will give in the evening, Kocham'ra.'

He began to walk. For the first time in his life he began to question his religion. Why had he joined the Church? Had it change anything in his life? He had always rejoiced in being a Christian. Like a caparisoned elephant, he had felt a certain personal pride. His friends and kinsfolk were still like Thevan and Kandankoran. He and Outhachayan and Paulos were so much greater than the other lot! That one thought had intoxicated Pathros on many occasions. But in the eyes of the ancient Christians he was just Pathros Pelen.

A long time ago foreign missionaries had established the Hilltop Church. The idea of conversion was not the only thought that had filled those hearts. They had aimed at the spiritual and material growth of the downtrodden people of that land. Years went by. India gained freedom. With that, several missionary organizations became independent. Today the original unity no longer existed in the Church. It had ruptured. The upper-caste Christians could never view the Pulaya Christians as their brothers. They were not willing to discard their ancestry. How could they give up their precious and ancient ancestry?

An internal struggle had begun in the Church on top of the hill between the Pulaya Christian and the Syrian Christian.

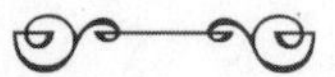

The time for harvest had arrived. The green paddy fields acquired a golden hue from the grain that adorned each plant. From the slope of the hill on which the Church stood, the cluster of fields lay outspread, a vast expanse. The early morning sun dripped more gold on the golden rows of grain. The dark-skinned women, carrying newly sharpened sickles, could be seen moving in a line along the edge of the fields. Thevan Pulayan stood in the Pallithara yard and watched.

He felt a sharp stab of pain as though a dagger had pierced his chest. The paddy field that lay snug on the other side of the line of fields was Narayanan Nair's, Thevan Pulayan's merciless Tham'ran's. Thevan was the one who had built its boundary, plied the seven-leafed wheel to dry out the excess water, and sowed the seeds. His sweat had fallen on that soil, drop by drop. His soul that had been plucked out and thrown away from that field was striking against its skeletal frame, crying to be let out.

'*Eda k'datha*, Kandankora,' Thevan Pulayan turned towards the house and called.

Kandankoran reached his Achan's side. The older Pulayan said, a sob in his voice, '*Eda k'datha*, harvest has begun.'

'*Hmm.*' A deep grunt. Kandankoran felt a grief-stricken sigh stifle his chest. He, too, was chewing down the pain.

Thevan Pulayan said, '*Eda k'datha*, they must be harvesting our field too.' Kunjol Velathan and son Azhakan, who were tenanting Anjilthara, must be moving towards the field now. He must reach there before that. Thevan was the one who sowed that field. The right to cut the first grain-laden shoot was his. He would not allow another to usurp that right.

'I'll go there and be back soon.'

Kandankora stopped him. Thevan would be inviting danger if he went there. Thevan Pulayan would not stand on the side and look on. He would enter the field and harvest. Thampuran would then use his stick on him. As the picture rose in his mind, Kandankoran felt a flash of fear. In earlier times workers often suffered the beatings of landlords.

'Acha, don't go.'

Thevan Pulayan experienced the agony that the soul of an imprisoned man feels. Kandankoran stood by silently. Life had no stability anywhere. It shifted beneath their feet. In those aimless lives, defeats outnumbered everything else. There might have been others among Thevan Pulayan's ancestors who had been thrown out of their homes in the same manner. Even then they had continued to serve the landlords. They showed great enthusiasm in seeing the landlord's granary fill with grain. Even as they worked themselves to death, the landlords grew stout. But they forgot that another generation had sprung from among the low castes and was growing up.

Unknown to Kandankoran, Thevan Pulayan went to the field. He walked fast—past Anjilthara, past the outer fence—but his legs were trembling. The tremor spread all through his body. Was that resistance? Maybe. It could also be the weight of humiliation. The western wind blew in from Aayirampara field. Thevan Pulayan inhaled deeply. As he inhaled the air, he felt a new life enter him.

People were already lined up in the field. Kunjolu Velathan from Anjilthara cut the first crop. The others too began to reap and move forward. Thevan Pulayan could not bear to watch it.

The old Pulayan turned and walked back.

13
Harvest

The Mission had its own paddy field. The parish priest was in charge of harvesting that land. The new Christians who tenanted the Mission land harvested the crop. That was the custom. Pallithara Pathros led the harvest as head Pulayan. Outha Pulayan would arrive, carrying a folded *puttil,* to pluck the odd paddy shoot that escaped the sickle. Squatting and crawling, the old man would gather the grain from the ground. Paulos and his wife would also come. During that time, Custodian Thomas would arrive as the priest's representative. He would sit on the edge of the field in the shade of a coconut tree, holding an umbrella.

This year, too, the crop in the field ripened, the grain-laden stalks bent sideways. It was nearing the twilight hour when Custodian Thomas called out from near the graveyard, 'Pathros Pelen'e, tomorrow is the day for harvesting the Mission field.'

'O.' Pathros answered respectfully. He told Maria, 'Did you hear, *edi*? Tomorrow at dawn, we need to go to harvest the crop.'

Placing a worn towel on his shoulder, Pathros went out quickly. He must inform Outha Pulayan, Paulos, and the others, else it would be wrong. When there was paddy to be got from harvesting the Church's land, all the new Christians claimed a share; they would be offended if they were left out. Everyone had a right to it. It was not for Pallithara Pathros alone.

Mother and daughter were alone in the house. For some time now a desire had filled the depths of Anna *kidathi*'s heart. She could not suppress it. She had to say it. Anna *kidathi* told her mother, 'Ammachi, when we go to harvest the field we'll call Kandankorachayan too.'

Maria had thought about it too. But unlike her daughter it was not born of affection. Thevan and son had been staying in Pallithara for almost two months. During that time Kandankoran had gone out on daily-wage labour four or five times. Apart from that they had not contributed any money towards household expenses. If two Kuttanadan Pulayar went to harvest they would get at least ten measures of grain to keep aside in the *puttil*. Maria thought it all out in an instant. Yet, when Anna *kidathi* spoke about calling Kandankoran for the harvest, she was disturbed. There had been a tremor in her daughter's voice; did it not suggest that love throbbed in her heart?

Maria asked in a scolding tone, 'What is it to you, *k'dathi*? Look at her talk, a full-grown girl. Kandankorachayan! Who is he, *edi*?'

Her mother had understood her feelings. Older, experienced people could guess a lot from the expressions and words of a girl like her. Anna *kidathi* felt shy. Unwilling to admit, she managed to say, 'What's with you, Ammachi?'

Now Maria became really angry. Truly, there were enough reasons to get angry, weren't there? A young man had come to stay in a house where there was a grown young woman. There was no sign of his leaving any time soon. All that irritation came out in one sentence from Maria: 'Girl, be careful.'

As though she agreed with the warning, as though she had submitted to it, Anna *kidathi* remained silent. Her heart had been stolen. She had forgotten her own self. Even for a moment she could not refrain from day-dreaming about that handsome ink-black man. Was that Anna *kidathi*'s fault? She was at an age where one could dream with eyes wide open. It was an ecstatic feeling that she could not shake off even if she tried.

Her daughter's posture, her engrossed look, shocked Maria. All said and done, was she not a mother? Would not the one who gave birth feel this anxiety? Gathering all her strength Maria snarled, '*Phha* ... What are you thinking, *edi*?'

Startled, Anna *kidathi* sat up. She looked rueful. Maria told her, 'Sharpen the sickle.'

Anna *kidathi* placed the pounding rod on a stone, sprinkled some powdered stone on it, and began to sharpen the sickle. Sparks flew as she pressed the sickle down, and moved it back and forth. After a while the curved mouth of the sickle shone like silver. Maria said, 'That is enough. Now go get the *puttil* and put the sickle in it.'

Anna *kidathi* obeyed. Maria was serving breakfast. She put Pathros's share into a bundle. She had to take it to the field as Pathros had left early. Maria said, 'Call Thevachayan.'

Anna *kidathi* went towards the veranda. There was no one there. The mat on which Thevan slept stood rolled up in one corner. Wonder when he had left! Kandankoran, too, was not to be found. The sharp words that Amma uttered from time to time might have hurt the poor man. If that was so, it was horrible. Anna *kidathi* looked out into the world outside. The sunlight was becoming warmer. When she thought of Kandankorachayan going out in that growing heat without food ... Oh, she felt like weeping. She could not bear the pain ... If she could only lay aside that heavy feeling.

Maria worked quickly. Harvest time had arrived. No work could be done in a leisurely manner. Her mind was like simmering water; it did not stay steady in any one place. Maria placed rice and curry on the tip of a leaf, and began to shape it into a packet. She tied it. She placed the sickles and the packet in the *puttil*, served her daughter rice, and said, 'Eat quickly, *k'dathi*.'

She couldn't. Anna *kidathi* just couldn't swallow the rice. How could rice go down her throat? She said quietly, 'I don't want any, Ammachi.'

Maria was annoyed. 'Oh is that so! What will you do, *k'dathi*? You have to reap till dusk, I tell you.'

But Anna *kidathi* refused to eat. Her heart was aching from a nameless pain. Quickly swallowing her food, Maria muttered, 'Your fate!'

They did not speak as they walked towards the field. The daughter's heart was weighed down by a sense of pain. They soon reached the Mission-owned field. As always Custodian Thomas was present on the ridge. The wheels of the spiritual and material progress of the Hilltop Church ran through that man's head. He looked so serious. Without lightening his gravity, he said to the Pulaya women, 'Walk quickly, *pennale*, it's time to harvest.'

Maria and daughter stepped down into the field. Pathros, Paulos, and Outha Pulayan's son, Azhakan, were there. In a black-edged checked *mundu* and a sleeveless vest, and his hair neatly cropped, Azhakan looked handsome. A hairline moustache, imported from some Tamil cinema, appeared above his upper lip. He stared at Anna *kidathi*, then smiled. The girl turned away, as though she found it unbearable.

Harvest began. They started reaping from the eastern corner of the field. The heavily-laden golden grain hung down beautifully. They moved forward striking at the neck of the golden shoots. Pathros stood at the edge of the field. Maria next to him. Anna *kidathi* stood to her southern side. It was a long row. Even as they enthusiastically reaped the paddy and moved on, pain lingered in a corner of Anna *kidathi*'s heart.

Outhachayan loved her like a father. She, too, had affection and respect for the old man. But that did not mean she would marry his handsome son. Even as he bent down with his sickle, Azhakan continued to look at Anna *kidathi* and smile. It annoyed her. What behaviour was this! She deliberately moved towards Maria and continued to reap, not looking to the left or right. Her thoughts wandered.

At noon they all climbed on to the edge and sat down, letting the perspiration cool. Stories were told, laughter rang out. Azhakan tried hard to catch Anna *kidathi*'s blue-tinged eyes and hold her glance. The eyes were, after all, the flowers that reflected the beauty of the heart. If you look into them you can see a person's inner life.

Outha Pulayan asked, 'Have you lost weight, my daughter?' The old man's words suggested too much affection.

Anna *kidathi* answered listlessly, 'O.' There was no warmth in her response.

The heat abated. The western breeze began to blow. The workers entered the field once again. All that time Anna *kidathi* had just one thought. Where had Kandankorachayan gone? What was he doing? She could find no answer.

That whole day Anna *kidathi*'s youthful heart pined for him. The sweet pain took hold of her heart.

In the evening as they walked towards the *thara*, Pallithara Pathros took a bundle of paddy sheaves and placed it in his *puttil*, which he tucked in his arm pit. Custodian Thomas saw it at once. His eyes reddened like those of the *uppan* bird. He angrily moved to Pathros's side and said, 'What is that, Pathros Pelen'e?'

Pathros was not upset. There was no reason to be upset. Why should he be worried or embarrassed? It was usual for the head Pulayan to take a bundle from the field to buy coffee, or a drink. That was his right. The Pulayan who produced the golden crop in the clay-filled field could take a bundle of grain without any offence. Pathros said, 'A bundle. So what?'

Custodian Thomas was furious. With the authority of a landlord he snarled, 'Put it down, *eda*. Pathros Pelen'e, put it down.'

'*Ho*!' Pathros grunted sarcastically and continued to walk. Maria and Anna *kidathi* followed him. There was no reason for Custodian Thomas to be so high-handed, particularly because the field was owned by the Mission. The crop had grown on the Mission field. What right did the Custodian have to speak in the tone of a landowner?

It was growing dark. Anna *kidathi* threshed the grain gathered in the *puttil* and sieved it to remove the husk. Maria lighted the stove with the dried end of a coconut leaf. Anna *kidathi* fried the grain and pounded it in the stone ural. It was time to get supper ready.

Pathros stepped out into the yard and told Maria, I'm going to the Church.'

Maria asked without enthusiasm, 'What for?'

'Today is committee meeting, Ammachi.' Anna *kidathi* had not forgotten it.

'I'll return soon.' So saying, Pathros left. His form disappeared farther down the path.

A while later, Outha Pulayan and Paulos arrived at the entrance and hooted. Paulos called out: 'Has Pathrochayan gone?'

'*Uvve.*' Anna *kidathi* replied. They, too, walked towards the Church. Then silence.

Anna *kidathi* murmured to herself, 'Kandankorachayan hasn't come yet.' She placed food for them in a clay bowl and placed it in the *uri*[1] that hung down from the roof. Wonder when they would come?

It became really dark. Kandankoran and Thevan arrived. They had been harvesting in the field next to Aayirampara. On the way back they had measured out some grain at a food stall and had had supper there. When she heard this, a terrible sadness filled Anna *kidathi*. Were they slowly growing apart? They might now leave their *thara* for some other place. The lord of her heart would go far away; she would never see him, he would never say a word to her.

Anna *kidathi* covered her face with her hands and began to sob.

Maria asked, 'Why are you crying, *k'dathi*?'

No answer to that. Anna *kidathi* continued to weep as though terribly hurt.

Maria went to the veranda and asked the visitors, 'Where did Thevachayan and son harvest?'

Thevan said in a tired voice, 'Far away. Next to Aayirampara.'

[1] A coir ring hung from the roof to hold pots and woks.

After a while Maria asked, 'Don't father and son want to eat?'

It was Kandankoran who replied, 'Oh, we don't want, Ammi. We had rice at a *choru kada* on our way back.'

Once harvest begins in Kuttanad, eateries come up near the outer fence, their sides covered with woven palm leaf. Lunch, coffee and snacks are available at all times. The Pulayar would gather one or two small measures of grain in their *puttil* as they left the field and go straight to the hotel. Maria knew this. She grunted, '*Hmm*. Now it's the time for harvesting and threshing! There will be rice.'

Anna *kidathi*'s heart trembled. Ammachi's words were loaded with meaning. They could pierce the heart like a poisoned spear. Thevan felt as though he had swallowed his tongue. A terrible moment. He had thought several times that he must leave Pallithara as soon as possible. It was a burden for Pathros, but it was not just that. Thevan had been born in a house where gods and deities were worshipped. Ritual killing of a cockerel was done every year in his *thara*. Even though they were all Pulayar, he felt suffocated in that shack. Like a boil atop a hunchback, Maria's dislike was increasing by the day. But where could the poor man go? Thevan's tired eyes moved towards the horizon. There was darkness everywhere. If only a spot of light would glimmer in that thickening gloom! The flush of twilight reflected by the rays of the setting sun was gone.

Thevan and son spread their mats, and lay down on the veranda. They felt orphaned in that house. It was a feeling that became more intense as each hour went by.

In the inner room Anna *kidathi* did not sleep. The jingle of her black bangles escaped through the woven holes and reached Kandankoran's ears intermittently. Time went by. The moon lay like a sliver of coconut in the sky, its face turned away. Kandankoran was not asleep. He lay watching the vast sweep of the night sky. The dim light of the moon pierced the thin cover of mist and spread all around.

It was past midnight when Pathros appeared. As they reached the entrance, Outha Pulayan and Paulos bid goodbye and left. In his hoarse trembling voice Outha Pulayan said, 'Now, at least, send them away.'

Kandankoran sat up on the mat. He was shocked. What was it that he had heard? Was it the kind of news he could hear and remain calm? The committee of the Hilltop Church had held an emergency meeting to discuss an important matter. He now understood what that matter was. People of another faith were staying in the true Christian Pathros's home. They were not leaving. Pallithara Pathros's house stood on land that belonged to the Mission. Therefore, the Church people could talk to him with authority.

Pathros lifted the woven screen door quietly and entered the room.

Maria asked softly, 'What was the meeting for?'

Pathros replied in an equally hushed voice, 'That … because Thevachayan and son are staying in our house.' Pathros stopped. He could not breathe.

Maria asked, 'Staying … Yes …?'

Pathros did not know how to explain it. Whichever way he explained, it would not be complete. He said, 'Achan said that Thevachayan and son should be sent away soon.'

A grief-stricken sigh escaped him. He said, a break in his voice: 'We are living on Mission land, aren't we?'

Anna *kidathi* lay awake thinking deeply. She could find no solution. She felt as though darkness had filled her life. She wept.

The dawn light spread. Thevan began to walk, the folded *puttil* in his armpit. Kandankoran hesitated for a moment, then went to Maria and said, 'Ammi, we are leaving.'

It sounded like a request. They had been given a mat and food in that house in their time of helplessness. He should thank her for that. That was what Kandankoran was doing. How could he not say at least that much? Was he not a man? Anna *kidathi* stood numbed. She had expected such a farewell. It was the right thing. But she had not expected it to happen so soon. The abruptness of that farewell pained her.

Maria said, listlessly bidding farewell, '*Enna poyatte* ... then go.'

Kandankoran turned and began to walk. His legs felt unsteady. His energy seemed to be draining. Perhaps he would never return to Pallithara.

Four or five days went by. As each day passed, Anna *kidathi*'s listlessness increased. The reason was unknown. It was harvest time. The time of prosperity in Kuttanad. It was the time that the Kuttanadan Pulayan could eat a bellyful of food. When all that they could see was the vast stretch of water that filled the fields, when the harsh western wind blew in the tiny coconut-tree filled inlands against the trembling shacks where the Pulayar crouched, shivering, they would say, 'Let harvest time come. Then we will eat.' The harvest time for which they had prayed had arrived at last. They could eat, drink, enjoy. At a time when tea stalls and hotels sprang up at the edge of every field Anna *kidathi* alone was unhappy. Maria could not bear it. Was she not a woman? She, too, had gone through that phase hadn't she? Anna *kidathi* was waiting for a young man, her heart full of pain. Wasn't that so? With the authoritative affection of a mother, Maria asked, 'What is this, *k'dathi*? What has happened to you?'

Anna *kidathi*, her face full of pain and her words tearful, bowed her head and said, 'Nothing.'

What else could she say?

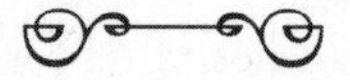

14
Conversion

One day Pathros came home, big with news. He announced, 'Our Azhakan *k'dathan* is going to join the Church.'

He took out the sickle tucked into the waist of his *mundu* and slid it between the woven panels of the wall. His face lit up with joy. One more baptism was about to take place in the Hilltop Church! That was not a small event! No, certainly not! That region was able to count another new Christian! The Church would receive a new Christian! But the reason for the joy on Pathros's face—that was something else.

Maria looked happy too. 'When is he joining the Church?' she asked, eager to know the day.

'The Sunday after next.'

The talk continued like an endless flowing stream. Azhakan would receive baptism early in the morning. The bishop *thirumeni*[1] and other dignitaries would come to perform that adult baptism. It was to be a grand event. Adoration would take place in the Church only after Azhakan had been baptized and initiated into the Church. The day was that important!

Maria thought about the special events of that day and rejoiced. She saw in her mind Azhakan getting baptized and joining the Church. Then, one day he would fasten the *minnu* around Anna *kidathi*'s neck ... Hopes grew in that manner.

Anna *kidathi* was not afraid. She had always known that this day would come. Azhakan would join the Church next Sunday. After

[1] *Thiru* means holy; *meni* means body. Bishops, like Brahmin priests, are called *thirumeni*.

that they would think about getting her married to Azhakan. The Christian Pathros would grunt his willingness. Outha Pulayan and Pathros were great friends. In the name of that friendship and to make it permanent, they would give her in marriage to Azhakan. That is what was going to happen. But she was not willing to sacrifice her desires.

Reaping and threshing were not yet over. Life in Kuttanad was heavy with labour. Throughout the day, even in the scorching heat that scattered the dry leaves, the poor reap and gather grain enthusiastically. At night—when a narrow streak of moonlight filters in through the mist, in the dim glow of lanterns—they thresh the grain into heaps on the threshing ground. That year's harvest was good.

Anna *kidathi* had no respite. No time even to sit down. Once she entered the field in the morning, she would leave it only at twilight. On the north-eastern side of the field, amidst the thick greenery that spread near the shore of the lake, was a pond. It was called Mundakkamoola. In the evening as she returned home, covered with hay dust, Anna *kidathi* would bathe in that pond. She used scented soap at that time.

It was Saturday afternoon. Maria, who stood in the line of reapers, straightened her back and said to her daughter in a kind voice, '*Edi k'dathi*, you have harvested enough. Go to the house now.'

Anna *kidathi* straightened up, surprised. This was a new experience. With the innocence of one who did not know what underlay the words, she asked, 'Why, Ammachi?'

Maria said in a gently scolding tone, 'Is it possible that you don't know? *Edi,* what day is today? Saturday. Tomorrow is Sunday. Tomorrow is Azhakan *k'dathan*'s baptism, isn't it?'

Anna *kidathi* stood with bowed head. What was she to do by going home this early? She could not find an answer. Finally Maria explained that as well: '*Adi k'dathi*, you go to the house quickly, and wash your *mundu*. Everyone in our *thara* must go to Church tomorrow.'

Anna *kidathi* began to walk. She had gone some distance when Maria called after her, 'Take two measures of grain from the *puttil* on the shelf and sell it in the shop. Buy soap or bluing … whatever."

Anna *kidathi* reached home. There was no one there. She entered the veranda and stood still. Two woven mats, neatly rolled up, leaned in the corner. They were Thevan Pulayan's and his son's. They had been standing, rolled up like this for quite a few days. Would they never be unrolled again? She took the *puttil* from the rack above the stove. Its mouth was shut tight. She unwound the cover, shook out some grain into a woven tray, and began to sift, to separate the chaff from the grain. Suddenly she remembered that her scented soap was all used up. If she took some more … Once again she took some grain, sifted it expertly, and measured it. She tied it up in a piece of cloth and walked towards the shop. This was a common thing in Pulaya homes. At harvest time there was ample grain in the *puttil*. They would measure it and take it to the shop to buy essentials.

Anna *kidathi* bought washing soap, bluing, and her scented soap, and began to walk home. The path lay deserted. Everyone was in the field. Lost in a day dream she did not know whether her footsteps were carrying her towards home. She opened the wrapper and smelt the soap. Ha! What an intoxicating fragrance! She walked a few more steps when suddenly she heard a call from behind.

'Anna *kidathi*!'

Startled, she turned and looked back. She could not believe her eyes. Her dear Kandankorachayan! She was so happy, she felt like weeping. He came up to her. 'Anna *kidathi*, where are you coming from?'

'I'm on my way back from the shop.'

Question and answer. Silence reigned. She had so many things to ask. He, too, had many things to ask. But no words emerged. After a while she said, 'I must go.' They moved away, farther and farther away. Anna *kidathi* reached home, bundled the clothes, and went to the pond. As she beat the *mundu* on the rock and washed it, emotions tumbled and echoed in her heart. Pearl-like teardrops fell on the wet *mundu*. She spread out the washed clothes to dry.

Idle thoughts moved across her mind like the silvery clouds that move along the sky driven by a light breeze.

It was Sunday. Azhakan wore a white shirt, patted back his thick curly hair, and arrived at the Church looking handsome. As the adoration went on and a long song was being sung, people guided him to the basin where baptism took place. The priest asked them to suggest a name. Authority vested with the godparents; Pallithara Pathros and Maria were the godparents. They responded to the priest's question, 'Mathai.' Achan took some holy water from the basin and poured it on Azhakan's forehead. With swiftness and ease, in a sing-song tone, as though reciting a poem, Achan said, 'Mathai, in the name of the Father, Son, and Holy Spirit, I baptize you. Amen.'

The crowd that pressed around them echoed like a beehive: 'Amen.'

The Hilltop Church had acquired yet another new Christian. The prayer over, people went their separate ways. As they walked back Paulos asked, 'Why do we join the Church like this?'

Pathros turned and asked gravely, 'What talk is that, Paulos'e?'

Old Outha Pulayan did not like that comment at all. Truly, Paulos had an evil eye. He was jealous because Outha Pulayan's son had joined the Church.

When he heard this Paulos was furious. He asked, 'Why should I be jealous?'

Thinking that a quarrel might erupt, Pathros intervened. There should not be a fight. He said loudly, 'Your tongue just cannot be controlled!'

Both men fell silent. But Outha Pulayan was still seething. Paulos was embarrassed. He had been misunderstood; Outhachayan had said to his face that he was jealous. No word had fallen from him to warrant that accusation. He had merely voiced his own experience. The upper-caste members of the Church had still not acknowledged the new Christians as equals. They denied them every right. When Custodian Thomas and the priest got together, every decision made by the new Christians dissolved and vaporized.

Paulos tried to control himself, but could not. He said, 'When I say something, you are displeased. So should I not talk? What I asked is, *why* do our people join the Church?'

Pathros realized what Paulos was trying to say. He was not just making accusations; there was truth in it. He was speaking from bitter experience. It was only natural to feel frustrated. Anyone would be, wouldn't they?

Did that poor lot have any say in the functioning of the Church? They should know what was happening. Custodian Thomas who came to oversee the harvesting of the Mission field—why did he come? Was it his own land that he should arrive holding a woven umbrella and give orders? It was not. It was the Mission's field. So even in the Church there was inequality based on caste. When low-caste folk became Christians, they still experienced exclusion. They were kept at a distance. Why was all this done if caste superiority existed within the Church? Was it not better that the Pulayar and Parayar did not join the Church?

Paulos said all this in his unpolished language. They were words that throbbed with pain. Pathros thought for a while and then asked, 'But how can we not join?'

Was that state better than this? Pathros was asking about life outside the Church. Weren't there *thampurans* and rich people there as well? Another point, Pathros's and Paulos's people were slaves over there.

But if the slavery continued even after conversion, wasn't that bad?

No one could find an acceptable answer to the question of conversion. Their selfhood had not grown that much. Without daring to say more on the subject, each went his way.

With the zeal of the new convert, Mathai came to Church every Sunday. The Custodian and the priest approved of him. When he saw them he stood up with great deference. Wiping the sweat off his tomato-round face with his large handkerchief, the parish priest said, looking at Mathai, 'Good lad.' There was no end to Outha Pulayan's joy when he heard this.

His godparents, Pallithara Pathros and Maria, too, had only good things to say about him.

What Anna *kidathi* expected to happen, with fear-tinged uneasiness, came to pass. One day a request for marriage arrived at Pallithara. Maria was so happy; if she could have made an offering of gold she would have done so. Could a mother experience greater joy? A good-looking and well-behaved young man had come, wishing to marry her daughter. Mathai was the groom. Mathai—old, irascible Outha Pulayan's son—who had been Azhakan once. Paulos, the boy's father, and two others came to finalize the wedding. The visitors sat in the veranda and narrated stories. Maria told her daughter, '*K'dathi*, you are lucky.'

Did Anna *kidathi* welcome that luck? She began to cry. To see her you would think someone had insulted her. Maria was startled for a moment. She asked, 'What is it, *k'dathi*?'

Anna *kidathi* sobbed, just sobbed. The tears upset Maria. Was she not a mother? She did not have six or a hundred children, all she had was this one child. If that child was hurt, her own heart would ache too.

Worried and anxious, Maria asked again, 'What is it, my daughter?'

Anna *kidathi* made no reply. Maybe she was wondering how to say, what to say. Pathros arrived. As soon as he came, he asked hurriedly, 'Who is going to the shop?'

Anna *kidathi* would have to go. If Maria went at such a time, nothing would happen well. So many things to be done! Taking the basket and handing it to her daughter, Maria said, '*K'dathi*, you go and return quickly.'

Anna *kidathi* had no complaints about that. She took the basket and went out through the back door to the road below. Pathros watched his daughter go. That strange grace that appears on a girl's face when she receives an offer of marriage had not blessed his daughter. There was no shy smile. She looked unhappy. She moved with legs that seemed too tired to carry her. Pathros asked, 'Why is *k'dathi* upset?'

Maria said casually, 'Oh, she's a child.'

Anna *kidathi* walked on. She could not believe her eyes. Kandankorachayan stood in front of her. She did not know which way he had come. When he saw her he stopped. She stopped too. He smiled but she did not. She could not smile. Isn't the face the mirror of the heart? Without feeling disheartened he called, 'Anna *kidathi*.'

She did not speak. Her eyes grew moist. He had never before called her with so much tenderness, with so much love. She felt her body trembling. Without smiling she bowed her head. Her stance made him feel cold. He asked in despair, 'Are you angry?'

Even then she did not speak. Her heart was aching as though it would break. He said, 'If you are offended, I won't say anything.'

Was she offended? Why should she be offended? People in love, who feel stifled by the sweet pain of love cannot quarrel and stay apart. If truth be told, she had so much to say. Did she not want to describe in detail … tell him how Azhakan had joined the Church, how he had changed his name and become Mathai. Not just that, he had come to her house with the desire to marry her.

She stood silently on the road that wound around the foot of the hill. He stood beside her. His love-filled eyes flitted over her beautiful body. She did not shrink. She was not the old shy Anna *kidathi*. There was a seriousness about her. There was no room for shyness.

After a while she raised her face and said softly, 'People have come to the house with an offer of marriage.'

He looked shocked as though he had never expected such a thing to happen. Barely conscious he asked, 'Who has come?'

Her heart burdened with pain and fear, Anna *kidathi* said, 'Azhakachan, our Outhachayan's son.'

His enthusiasm disappeared. Kandankoran felt cold. His lovely dream shattered to pieces. He stood as if he had been slapped hard.

Azhakan was a Christian now. He was a member of the Church. He was also not bad looking. Ink-black skin, curly hair, and a healthy body made him handsome. Kandankoran liked him. But that did not make his marrying Anna *kidathi* acceptable. But his likes or dislikes were of no worth. No one would ask his opinion. Could he marry her in his present condition? Was he worthy of it? No. Maybe if he, too, converted like Azhakan, it might be possible. But there were hurdles there as well. The first was Thevan, his father. He would not agree. Gods and deities were consecrated and worshipped in his *thara*. He could not join the Church with Thevan Pulayan's permission.

But to tie the *minnu* around Anna *kidathi*'s neck Kandankoran was willing to change his religion. He said, his face full of hope, 'I, too, will join the Church.'

She had been yearning to hear those words since such a long time. At last he had said it. She had heard it. After that she was afraid that he was joking. It was natural for a girl in her state to harbour such a fear. Had he understood the seriousness of joining the Church, of becoming a new Christian? She was confused, frightened. Her nerves felt racked, she felt as though she was suffocating.

He repeated, 'I, too, will join the Church. Then I'll tell Pathrochayan that I want to marry you.'

The words echoed in her ears. A Pulaya lad was saying this. He would join the Church so that he could marry her. When she thought about it a flush appeared on her cheeks. After a while she raised her face, her eyes filled with desire. Her eyes looked into his. She said, 'I must go.'

She went to the shop and returned. Maria was waiting for her anxiously. The grocery shop was not all that far. She should have been back by now. If she was late it meant she did not like the alliance. After all, the mother had seen tears falling like bits of glass from the blue-black eyes. When she thought of all this, the mother grew afraid. There were enough reasons for fear. As she waited anxiously, she saw the daughter coming. 'Can't you walk faster?' she asked.

But Anna *kidathi* continued to walk slowly. Maria took the basket and laid out the items on the floor, wondering if they would suffice.

There were special dishes to be served for the Kuttanadan Pulayan's lunch. Maria put her hand to her forehead and cursed.

'May those merchants rot!'

Anna *kidathi* pleaded, 'Speak softly, Ammachi.'

On the veranda, the conversation among the guests was in full swing. They had begun to discuss the wedding. Maria listened to it as she prepared food. She was relieved. When a grown daughter is in the house it is difficult to be calm. Anna *kidathi* was well-behaved. But she could go down the wrong path. A mother is at peace only when the grown daughter is married and sent off. Maria was also a mother.

One among the group said, 'So, that is decided. When is the wedding?'

'Next month.'

It was decided; Anna *kidathi*'s heart began to pound. All the dreams she had dreamt were falling apart. Now they might never become a reality.

Lunch over, the visitors chewed betel, spat out the juice, and departed. Anna *kidathi* told her mother, 'Ammachi, I don't want this marriage.'

'Why, *edi*?'

'I don't like it.'

Maria said angrily, 'If you start talking like this … What else do you want, *kidathi*?'

Anna *kidathi* sat with bowed head. There was something hidden in her heart. One could understand this from the way she sat, the way she looked. Maria understood.

'Then who do you like, *k'dathi*? Tell Ammachi.' Maria spoke in a gentler tone. Who else was there for her daughter to confide in, to open her heart to? Anna *kidathi* was in love. Her love was returned. The pain of love was weighing upon her heart. Till now she had never stepped away from the straight path. But that could happen. Before she stepped on to the wrong path, she must be married to the one who loved her.

The mother was coaxing her. She did not abuse or threaten. Didn't that mother have the ability to dig out the secret that was guarded so well?

Anna *kidathi* wanted to speak. If she did, the weight on her soul would lighten. She even shaped her tongue to utter the words. They might fall off her tongue any moment. Maria waited expectantly, but Anna *kidathi* did not speak.

As she sat without speaking, words echoed in her mind. Dark Kandankoran stood before her and asked, 'Anna *kidathi*, shall I join the Church?' She shivered. What if she told her mother that?

'Ammachi, Kandankorachayan too is going to join the Church.'

Maria sat without moving, her face expressionless. Earlier when she had heard that Azhakan was going to join the Church she had laughed aloud with joy. So full of enthusiasm had she been! Shouldn't that joy be repeated? Or did that day's happiness mean something else? The day before Azhakan joined the Church, her mother had sent her away to wash her *mundu*. Maria was determined to attend that baptism smartly dressed. Anna *kidathi* had seen that enthusiasm. It was natural that she expected it to be repeated. But Maria sat without moving, silent, her face grave.

15
The Desire to Marry

Kandankoran, too, joined the Church. He, too, acquired a new name. His name was Thoma. Apparently, that name appeared in the holy book of the religion he had joined! Thoma felt very proud.

One day when he said, 'My name is in the holy book,' Paulos burst out laughing. How could he not laugh? The folly of that sentence! Not knowing the reason, Thoma asked, 'Why are you laughing, Achaya?'

Paulos said with the look of a seasoned Christian, '*Eda k'datha*, listen. You will feel this way now. All our names are from the holy book.'

That was a staggering piece of information. All the Christian names were in the holy book! Paulos was emphatic. The priest was not being partial when he gave him the name Thoma. It was just one of the names in the Bible. An upper-caste Christian *thampuran*, Custodian Thomas, had the same name. Poor Thoma thought that the name was exclusive to him. The thought had had an intoxicating effect on him. And now, Paulos was saying this! Thoma's enthusiasm dulled a bit. Paulos, Mathai, Pathros, all of the names, the weight of which the new Christians bore, were from the Bible.

When Thevan Pulayan heard that his son had joined the Church, the old man trembled with fury. He had not expected such a thing to happen. Sacrificing roosters and drum-beating used to take place regularly in Anjilthara. There were famous *velathans* among Thevan Pulayan's ancestors. Because Thevan Pulayan worked in a paddy field, because he became the head Pulayan in Narayanan Nair's vast Aayirampara field, these practices had been halted. He had in his safekeeping, even now, the conch shell and cowries that his forefathers had used. That father had hoped that his son would carry on the tradition.

All those hopes were dashed in a single moment. His son changed his religion, that too for the sake of a girl. Did he have to change his religion just because he was struck by her beauty? Was there no other way?

'From now on he is not my son,' said Thevan Pulayan bitterly.

The old man bent his thin face covered with grey stubble, resting it on his arm. The rough voice repeated, 'He is no longer my son.'

But Thoma knew nothing of this. He was in the ecstasy of love. He saw a girl, succumbed to her smile, surrendered his heart. He would do anything to marry her—her alone. There was no point in finding fault with him.

One day they met on the edge of the field as she was returning from the threshing ground. There was a bundle of paddy on Anna *kidathi*'s head. She was walking with difficulty under the weight of that load. Thoma, who came from the opposite side, saw her. He could not bear the sight. She worked so hard!

'Anna *kidathi'ye*, I'll carry it.'

She did not refuse. Had she not chosen this man to shape her very life, to mould their future together? Then why should she be embarrassed? He took the load and began to walk in front with perfect ease. To see him walk, you would think he did not know he was carrying a load on his head. Or was he bearing the heavy weight smilingly for the girl he loved? Perhaps. Maybe it would not seem heavy then.

'When is the wedding?' he asked, continuing to walk.

That question shook her. It was true, wasn't it? The wedding was planned for the next month. He could make a decision only if she told him. Truly, that was what she wanted to tell him. But could a girl say it? She was in a dilemma.

'Anna *kidathi*, finally I joined the Church; for what, to marry you!'

Perhaps due to his anxiety, his throat went dry. He fell silent. He could not continue to talk in that manner. A desire that had lain hidden for a long time had now been expressed. What more could he say?

'Come home and tell Achan.'

'I will.'

They climbed the steps of the Hilltop Church and walked down to the canal near the graveyard. She could not make him carry the bundle any further.

'I'll take the bundle and go ahead.'

He agreed and placed the bundle on her head. He wiped his streaming face. At that time he remembered what the parish priest had said: 'The Lord God says you must eat by the "sweat of your brow".' He felt he was standing before that eternal command like a humble servant. Thoma raised his tired eyes and looked up. The Church stood facing the horizon, bearing the cross aloft.

'You walk ahead,' Thoma said.

He was alone now. After a while he must go to Pallithara. Tell them everything. There was nothing to be ashamed of in asking for a girl. But there were some conventions to be followed. What right did the bridegroom have to go and ask for the girl? Shouldn't his guardian and other elders go, and ask for the bride?

When he thought of that, Thoma suddenly felt weak. But he could not escape his thoughts.

Who was there to speak for him? No one; his father was angry and had disowned him. Thevan had also become delusional. He sat in the shade of a coconut tree behind the outer fence of Aayirampara field with his ancestral conch and cowry shells. At one time they had lain on the shelf above the stove in his old *thara*, in an old disintegrated *puttil*, blackened by the smoke from the stove below. He had kept them secure as if saving them for the future. These days he sat drawing squares on the sand and placing shells in them with great concentration. He did it every day without fail. Thevan, who had lost everything, was holding on tightly to the heritage of his bygone ancestors, a tradition his one and only son had rejected.

Thevan, who was no longer in possession of his senses, would not go to Pallithara to discuss the wedding. Who else was there to go for him? Thoma felt that he was alone in that vast universe. Was that not true? In this world where thousands of men and women gave birth and multiplied, he had no one.

Filled with a sense of loneliness, he began to think of marriage even more intensely. Some time went by in that manner.

Thoma entered Pallithara all by himself.

The householder was at home. '*Hmm,* why have you come?' Pathros asked. His face looked dull. There was no enthusiasm.

Though the answer 'Just like that' arose in his throat, Thoma did not say it. It would be a weak reply.

He tried to speak. His lips moved in anticipation of it. But words did not emerge. Thoma's face twitched in that frustrated attempt. He entered the veranda with unsteady steps, feeling vulnerable. It was a floor that had welcomed him some time before.

'*Hmm,* why have you come?'

A totally unwarranted anger seemed to throb behind that question. Or was it just Kandankora's imagination? When someone comes to the house and sits down, the householder has to say something. That was his duty. Wasn't this, too, an exercise of formality?

A few more minutes went by in that manner. Anna *kidathi* stood inside, holding her breath, her heart beating unusually fast. She was waiting. Yes, she was waiting.

Why was Thoma not saying it? Was he wondering how to broach the subject? At least he had the surety of her love. Did it not lend him strength? She was afraid that the silence would never end. Wasn't it natural for a girl in her position to be afraid? She was promised to another young Pulayan, Mathai. But in her heart there was no place for anyone but Thoma.

'I desire to marry Achan's daughter.' Could he not begin in that manner? From there words would flow with ease. The lengthening silence frightened her. Minutes went by. Finally, Thoma said hoarsely, his throat dry, 'I want to marry Anna *kidathi*.'

Havoo! Though his voice broke, he had managed to complete that sentence. Didn't that short sentence contain an entire love story? Like the scenes reflected in the clear water of the forest stream, did it not reflect the love of two young hearts? Could this story be told with greater clarity and fullness?

Pathros did not reply. Would that plea go unheeded? Pathros's silence confused and worried Thoma. Pathros had to give him a reply. Only then could Thoma think of the next sentence. Anna *kidathi* somehow managed to stand within the room. She was sweating profusely; her bodice, her bud-like cheeks, her forehead, were all bathed in sweat. The beautiful half-moon-like forehead grew moist. A feeling of frenzied breathlessness came over her. She felt as if she was standing on live coal.

Pathros's silence was not auspicious but that deliberate silence could not last. It would crack soon. When a father is asked for his daughter's hand in marriage—particularly when he knows that the man is loved by his daughter—how can he not reply? Did Thoma have any obvious deficiency that he could point out? When he looked at the young man, Pathros definitely felt that he had deficiencies but he could not quite explain what they were. All he knew was that he wanted a 'better boy' for his daughter. But Pathros did not really know what that 'better' meant.

Pathros said, '*K'dathan* came and asked for the girl. That is as it should be. There is nothing wrong in that. But …'

It ended on a note of dissatisfaction. But Thoma felt relieved. His request had not been rejected outright. It had been accepted; not just that, its relevance was admitted. When he said 'That is as it should be', what else did that father mean? But that alone was not enough. Pathros's reply had ended on an inconclusive note.

'What is the problem, Achan?' Thoma asked humbly.

Pathros nodded. He must say it. He asked, 'Where will you live with the girl?'

Thoma lowered his head. Pathros had pointed out a serious drawback. If he wanted to marry a girl there should be a home where he could live with her. Thoma, who did not have a home of his own, had no answer.

But he was not disheartened. There were very few Pulayar who had land of their own. For the Pulayan, the land he stood on was everything. Maybe, if some landlord permitted, he could build a shack near some outer fence. Even the salt-laden west wind that blew fiercely from across the sea could not damage a Pulaya shack. It was that strong. The homes of landlords might collapse, but Pulaya homes never did. Thoma would build a home beside some *thampuran*'s outer fence. Was that a problem for a Pulayan?

Not just that, when Pathros married Maria, did he have a home of his own? He had built that house on Mission land some twenty years ago. Before that he had stayed in different shacks built on the land of different *thampuran*s on whose lands he had worked. That was his history. Thoma had joined the Hilltop Church. Baptismal water had fallen on his forehead too. According to practice he, too, could build a house on Mission land. The Church allowed it. As for savings, who among the Pulayar had any? Perhaps a few might be saving money. Why should Thoma save? He was the inheritor of the many hundreds of golden grains that sprang up in the fields. If you thought about it, weren't those clusters of fields really his?

'I will build a house and live there,' he said gravely, looking Pathros in the face.

There was a determination in those words which Anna *kidathi* heard. He was talking about the plans he had formed about life. Build a house. Live there. Anna *kidathi* looked towards the eastern side of the Church. There was enough land there to build another shack. The ones who had newly joined the Church could build their homes there. The committee had taken such a decision. She had heard Pathros mention it.

She wanted to enter the conversation, which lacked momentum, to say, 'We'll live on Mission land and build a house.' But could she say it? If she said that one sentence, the conversation that now sagged would become taut again. With new energy Thoma could ask for her. Now he looked anxious. He was not saying anything.

Like one desperately trying to avert another defeat, Thoma said, 'I will build a house.'

It was possible. It could happen; it might not take all that much time too. One needed just ten or fifteen rupees to make a house. If you gave a written promise to do Onam work, any *thampuran* would give that amount. True, there were some defects in that relationship, but Thoma was a nice lad, a loving lad.

Pathros was a father. That father could not casually dismiss one who had come with a request for his daughter's hand. He said, 'Come next week, *k'datha*. I'll talk to you then.'

Thoma began to walk away. He walked towards the path near the cemetery, then turned and looked back. Anna *kidathi* stood watching him. Their eyes met. It was an intense look. He began to walk again.

16

Thoma's Petition for a Home

Thoma did not know how the idea popped up in his head. It was a miracle. When Pathros had asked him where he would live, he did not have a proper answer. All that he could manage to say was, 'I'll make a house and live there.' But then he realized he could build a house on Mission land and live there! First he had to write an application; then submit it before the committee. Thoma knew several families that had been baptized and then built homes on Mission-owned land. All the mud shacks scattered around the Hilltop Church had come up in that manner.

He made his decision. Wonder how that idea had come to his mind! At a time when necessity had loomed, when that sense of urgency had forced him to think incessantly, the solution suggested itself.

Thoma went to the junction and bought a sheet of paper for an *anna* from the wayside shop. Now he must prepare an application. Its form lay within him. He just had to breathe it out into sentences, give life, get them written. The application should have vitality. It should have the power to touch the hearts of the committee members. Who was there who would write it for him? He had entered the clay of Kuttanadan paddy fields when he was five. Besides, the Pulayan whose brain lay like a desert was denied education in those days.[1]

[1] The Pulayar were thought to be bare of intelligence, as per the general perception. They were thought to be fit only for manual labour.

He stood holding the roll of white paper. There were several people around him who could write. But would they write for him? He waited for some time. No one came that way. Lots of people walked along that road every day. But today, of all days, no one came by. He went to Pillaichan's tea shop.

'What is it, Kandankora, I don't see you these days.' Those were Pillaichan's welcoming words.

Laughter arose from among the people who sat in the crowded tea-stall. One of them said, 'He's not Kandankoran now.'

'Then?'

'He's Thoma. He joined the Church. He's a *kristyani*.'

The man said it in a manner that made it sound that it was all a lie—that his name was not Thoma, that he had not joined the Church, that he was not a Christian either. It was the truth, wasn't it? Then why wouldn't the man accept it? His tone was soaked in sarcasm. He was mocking Thoma.

Thoma felt a surge of anger. He asked angrily, 'What is there to laugh at? Am I not a '*krityani*'?[2] Did I not join the Church?'

Again, there was a burst of laughter. The man who had made the comment said, 'Yes, *eda*, you are a *poocha kristyani*, a fraud.'

Poocha kristyani! Thoma was stunned. He had every right to be shocked, didn't he? So what if the Pulayan receives the Christian faith, if the holy of holies baptizm water falls on his forehead, if a cross is drawn on his forehead, if he gets a new name? All that does not change his *pula*, his untouchable status. Indeed, what a cursed creature he was!

The excitement that had spurted within him died. He cringed as though he had been thrashed. He had been humiliated in the presence of so many people! He had destroyed his inheritance. Did a new Christian have an identity of his own? Would society acknowledge it? That term, *poocha kristyani*! The mocking laughter

[2] The new religion is so alien that Thoma doesn't even know the correct term, 'kristyani'.

that followed it! He could not forget it. His heart burned. He would never know peace again.

Thoma's face paled. All those gathered there saw it. Pillaichan felt sorry for him. He decided to make his sympathy known. He said, 'The poor Parayan and Pulayan are allowed to join the Church; then they are called frauds. … All this goes against God, remember.'

The words uttered in a stern voice were too much! If anyone should be insulted, it should be that Thoma Pulayan. He is the one who should feel ashamed. It was he who was called a fraud. Pillaichan should not have taken his side. A tea-stall owner was needed by all. And he must please everyone. Pillaichan should not have forgotten that.

A Syrian Christian who sat at the head of the bench jumped up. He said, 'Why, Pillaicha, why are *you* hurt? If we said something, it was to the Pulayan we admitted into our Church. What is it to *you*?'

Pillaichan had not expected such a reaction. But it had happened. In truth, it was not a subject he should have talked about. However, he could not concede defeat. He was a man who had never experienced defeat in his life. Raising his voice he countered.

'Why are *you* upset? Can you stop me from talking?'

That was a challenge. Perhaps a fight might start. An elderly person intervened. 'Stop, Pillaichan and Mathai *mapp'la*, both of you stop. How can you be so senseless?' The old man chewed betel, spat out into the sand-laden yard, and said, 'You can stop the mouths of a thousand pots but you cannot shut a man's mouth.'

Mathai could not withdraw defeated. The man wanted to utter the last word.

'Pillaicha, we might allow or not allow Pulayar to join our Church. You need not interfere in it.'

There was accusation in those words. It sounded as though Pillaichan did not favour Pulayar joining the Church! The words hinted as much. Was that the truth? Pillaichan had seen Thoma's wilted face. He had reacted to it instinctively. Was it right to insult one who had been baptized, call him a fraud to his face without any pity, and then laugh contemptuously? That was all that Pillaichan had intended to say. He never dreamt such an interpretation could be given to his words.

To put an end to Mathai's tongue, he said, 'You need not advise me. I know you well.'

Mathai said, dismissing the words, 'What is there for you to know?'

He took out his purse out of the folds of his *mundu*, jingling the coins loudly. Taking a few coins, Mathai turned towards Pillaichan and asked, 'How many *annas, edo*? I'm not coming to your coffee shop again.'

Taking the money Pillaichan said sarcastically, 'Oh my shop won't run if you don't visit it. Didn't you all know? I'm closing down the shop and leaving.'

In this manner, in the name of a new Christian, an argument arose in the middle of the road. People split up, joining one side or the other. Mathai went straight to see Custodian Thomas and described the incident. The Custodian's face reddened when he heard it. Sweat beaded the tip of his nose. Together, the two of them told every Syrian Christian sternly, 'None of you should go to Pillaichan's tea-stall again.'

All this time Thoma, who had been ridiculed as a fraud, stood waiting on the veranda of the tea-stall. The thing that he had come for had not yet happened. The rolled-up sheet of paper was still in his hand. Who would prepare a request for him?

Pillaichan asked, 'What are you waiting for, Kandankora?'

Thoma was embarrassed. Pillaichan said, 'You may have joined the Church, but I will always call you Kandankora. Did you hear, *da*?'

'*O*.' Thoma agreed humbly.

Pillaichan repeated the question, 'Do you want coffee or something?'

What Thoma wanted was not coffee. He had a greater need. He wanted to build a home. A home of his own, so that he could get married and live there. That tender desire, innate to the human heart, was growing within him. The foundation for it lay in the letter that was to be prepared and presented before the committee members of the Church. Who would render that invaluable service for him? Thoma explained all this to Pillaichan.

'Please prepare an application for me. I'll never forget that kindness.'

His voice broke. His eyes filled with tears. He would be grateful for all time to the man who wrote that application for him, which he could submit to the committee. What more could Thoma promise?

'All that is true,' Pillaichan replied. 'But will the Church folk give you land to be a tenant, Kandankora?'

Thoma had no doubts about that. He recited the names of the owners of the mud huts that lay scattered around the Hilltop Church. All those houses had taken shape in that manner, he confirmed. Then would they deny that to him alone?

Pillaichan said, 'All right, you come at night after ten o'clock. I'll have customers till then.' The teachers in the government school nearby had their night meal from the shop. He had to serve them rice. Pillaichan would be free only after that.

Thoma got out into the yard. Pillaichan called, 'Just wait, Kandankora.'

That call was an irritation. Everyone called him by that name, at least for now. Perhaps they had got used to it. Perhaps the name came unconsciously to their lips. But each time he heard that call, Thoma squirmed. The new enthusiasm, the sense of pride that had awakened in him, suffered a jolt. No one seemed to understand that. His heart was aching.

Thoma turned and looked back. Pillaichan asked, 'Can you cut two logs for me? I'll give you food.'

You can give a Pulayan belly full of rice and make him do any work. Tea-stall owner Pillaichan was a representative of the upper-caste people who made Pulayar work in that manner. Thoma had to obey. He asked humbly, 'Where is the wood?'

It was at the back of the tea-stall. As he walked, axe against his shoulder, he thought, 'It's very heavy.' There, behind the tea-stall, blocks of wood lay in a pile. He felt dazed when he saw them. Thoma lifted each one of the blocks, placed it at an angle, and began to hack at it with the heavy axe. He thought to himself, 'Wonder when I'll finish chopping all this wood.'

But he could not excuse himself. He must chop all those blocks of wood. Streams of sweat flowed down Thoma's chest. He panted. Even then the axe in his hand continued to rise and fall.

Did a poor man like him have the right to complain? Very few of his desires in life had been met. Even for the few that had materialized, he had had to render so many services. Too many. Too many. In spite of all this, Thoma had no complaints. He had never learned to complain. Perhaps, if he did complain, no one would pay attention either. Who knew?

Thoma's arms began to ache. It was not a job he was used to. He had harvested in the field. He had threshed the shoots of paddy, separating grain and chaff. He had dived into the lake to gather clay and unloaded it on to the ridge. But he was not familiar with chopping wood.

Finally, it was over. He entered the shop, streaming with sweat. It was a quarter to ten at that time. Pillaichan was lying back in his chair, reciting lines from the Bhagavatham. He stopped, turned his head sideways, and said, 'Let that school teacher come. He'll come for supper now. My handwriting is not good.'

Thoma thought, 'I should have gone to that teacher in the beginning itself. Had I done so, I wouldn't have had to chop all that wood!'

After a few minutes, the school master arrived.

He began to write the application. 'To be presented before the honourable committee of the Hilltop Church.' He stopped. Now he had to write the applicant's name and address. Thoma had just a name. He did not have an address. Could they write Thevan Pulayan, who had been a labourer in Narayanan Nair's Aayirampara field? No, that was not possible. That story was over. Today Kunjol and family lived in Anjilthara. They could not write 'Thevan's son, Thoma' either. So many blanks! Thoma was the owner of an unacknowledged identity and he did not have a distinct address. What a pitiful situation!

The teacher looked at the unfurled paper and said, '*Hmm*. Tell me quickly. I have to go.'

Thoma stood confused. How should he explain? There was justification in the teacher's exhibition of haste. Thoma's dilemma, too, was understandable. Thoma said tentatively, 'My name is Thoma.'

The teacher shook his head, 'That is not enough, Thoma. When you write a letter, you need a definite address.'

Thoma said with bowed head, 'I do not have a home. That is why I am making you write the request.'

His throat dried up. Words became unclear. It seemed as though tears would start dropping from his tired eyes. The teacher thought for a while, then asked, 'When did you join the Church?'

Thoma replied quickly, 'The previous month of Thulam, the twenty-fifth day.'

The teacher first wrote the year, then the month and date. 'Thoma, who was baptized in the Hilltop Church on that day, hereby wishes to inform …' Pillaichan liked the sentence. He expressed his appreciation: 'Good. That is good.'

The application was written. A neat copy was prepared. As he received it, Thoma felt his heart would burst with the burden of gratitude. A sort of sentence came out of his parched throat, 'Tham'ran, you're kind.'

The teacher looked at him with a smile. 'Thoma, do not call me Tham'ran. I do not like it.'

Those words echoed in Thoma's ears. There were people like this! Was he a human or a god? This man was so much greater than the tea-stall owner Pillaichan or Custodian Thomas. He called them all Tham'ra. They all revelled in the joy of hearing that obsequious term. It pleased them to hear it. But this teacher from the school was different. He rejected it!

Thoma took the application and quickly stepped on the road. He walked with long strides. What a rush! Pillaichan called after him, 'Are you leaving without eating?'

Thoma did not want anything. He just wanted to somehow reach the Mission bungalow and submit the application to the parish priest. He tried to walk faster. He was panting. The road to the bungalow looked like it would never end!

An electric lamp shone in the glass window pane of the Mission bungalow. The priest had not slept yet. Under the circle of light, with his head raised against a silken pillow, he must have been reading some holy text. Thoma lengthened his stride.

He reached the bungalow and gave the application to the priest.

The next day at the top of the road he saw Custodian Thomas.

'Did you give an application?'

'O, I did.'

'Why did you not ask me? Insolence!' the Custodian snarled.

Thoma did not reply. What was he to say? That new Christian did not know that he had to get the Custodian's permission first. There were so many things he had to learn!

He began to walk away.

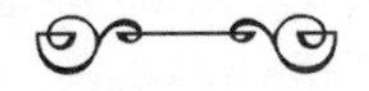

17

Pathros Agrees to the Wedding

There were heated arguments at the committee meeting of the Hilltop Church. Finally, Thoma's application was accepted; he was granted permission to build a home on Mission land. His heart throbbed with sheer joy. He began to build the house with the help of some friends.

Within three days the work was complete. A frame of thick and thin bamboo stumps, tightly bound together, were held up by four pillars. When this was covered with woven coconut palm leaves, the shack looked like a mushroom that had sprung up from the ground.

Anna *kidathi* stood watching it all. The joy in her heart was growing. The chariot of her dreams was moving forward. Her desires began to blossom once again. There was no reason for despair.

Once again Thoma came to Pallithara. This time Maria was in the house. Anna *kidathi*'s heart was beating uncontrollably. Would Pathros reject Thoma's request with one '*okkathilla*', 'not possible'? Maria was not in favour of the marriage.

'Why don't you say something, Achan?'

Pathros asked, 'Will *k'dathan*'s achan agree?'

Poor Thevan Pulayan was devastated when his son joined the Church. That defeated and heartbroken old man now wandered along the outer fence of Aayirampara field holding onto his sole inheritance, his conch and cowry shells. He rattled the shells, drew squares on the sand, and tried to understand the constellations. How could such a man agree to his son marrying a new Christian's daughter?

Thoma said with bowed head, 'Achan might not agree.'

Immediately, Pathros asked, 'Then how can it be?'

Maria had something to say. She said, 'With no one else to come or to ask, I will not give the girl. I will not agree.'

The words echoed in Thoma's ears like some terrible curse. It seemed as though an unknown force was saying, 'We will not give you Anna *kidathi*.'

'Why do you have to interfere? Why?' Pathros asked, displeased.

'Am I not talking sense?'

'Yes, you talk sense. Now be silent.'

Maria went inside. That was good, because there Anna *kidathi*'s tear-filled eyes greeted the mother. Sobbing, she said, 'Ammachi, I want this.'

'*Entemole*, my daughter, do not fall for that *k'dathan*'s looks. He has no one of his own.'

Anna *kidathi* replied with finality, 'What if I want it?'

'What did you say?'

'Just what I said.'

Maria thought for a while. She went to the door and called Pathros aside. She said, 'Did you hear what Anna *kidathi* said?'

'What is it?'

'That she wants this marriage.'

Pathros asked his daughter, 'Is it enough, *mole*?'

'It is enough, Acha,' she said as she wiped the tears that filled her eyes.

The affectionate father could not go against his daughter's desire. Pathros walked towards the veranda and said to the waiting Thoma, 'We will have the wedding.'

Thoma had not thought that a decision would be made so quickly. He was happy with that gracious blessing, so generously given. He asked, 'When will you have it, Acha?'

'Next month.'

Thoma began to walk. His face was bright, clear. He went and stood in front of the Church. The entire universe lay before him. The paddy fields and hilltops could be seen clearly in that light. He stood watching it all. White clouds moved idly across the sky like soft fluffy cotton balls.

18
Changes

New Christian Thoma's home could be seen, a mushroom-like outgrowth, on the eastern side of the Hilltop Church. He and his wife Anna *kidathi* were its inhabitants. There was laughter there; laughter and play and embraces that made them thrill all over. Their lives throbbed with vitality.

Every morning Thoma gulped down the black coffee that Anna *kidathi* boiled for him, and went to work in the vast cluster of fields. That was where his work lay. He was linked to the land which lay between the sticky clay embankments by the responsibilities that life laid down. His life was labour.

But that did not mean that Thoma was any *thampuran*'s Onam labourer. His father's experience had been a lesson for him. That tragedy should not be allowed to repeat itself. He worked for daily wages, collected his wage at the end of the day, and returned to his shack. From the long path that wound around the foot of the hill, Thoma would look up at his shack. In the fast-fading blush of the disappearing sunlight, his home was a speck. He would be in a hurry to reach it. He was proud of having a house of his own. Wasn't a love-filled heart waiting for him?

Emotions filled up and throbbed in that tiny home. Its inhabitants were dark-skinned but they, too, are human, are they not? The intense longing to thrill each other with repeated kisses, the desire to be one in a joyful embrace, the bliss and sweetness of union that extends to the inner depths of the soul; here, too, the raw innate passions of life were abundant.

Anna *kidathi* would prepare the night meal and wait for Thoma. The moment she heard his heavy footfall in the yard, she would hasten to the door and welcome her husband with a smile that lit up her face.

She would move into the arm that he stretches towards her and say, 'You look very tired today.'

Thoma would say, as though denying it, 'Not tired at all.' But she would not agree. He had been working in the harsh sunlight the whole day. He did not have a regular place of work. At times he went to till the tapioca crop on the slope of the hill. At other times he would go to build an embankment. Very rarely did he go to work in the paddy field. The sight of the vast fields spreading towards eternity made his heart ache. It felt like it would break. The memory of leaving that tiny home near the outer ridge, helpless and vulnerable, flashes across his mind. Forgetfulness had not blessed him.

Old Thevan Pulayan still wandered along the embankment with his conch and cowry shells. He drew squares in the soft soil and played the game of spreading cowry shells on them. It would continue in that manner—the unacknowledged repetition of the *velathan*'s ritual that he had inherited from his forefathers.

Thoma did not go to Pallithara. Not because he had any specific grievance against Pathros or Maria. They were, after all, the parents of the girl who delighted his heart. There was no reason to be angry with them. But he hesitated to go there. He had stayed there like a beggar at a time when he had nothing but the cloth he wore. Even the mat on which he slept belonged to the people of that house. Pathros must have suffered many a hardship for him and the old man.

But Anna *kidathi*'s mother was not a good woman. That tongue had moved frequently, spewing caustic remarks. He remembered what Maria had once said, 'How can there be rice or anything else in the house? All we have is spent on feeding guests, is it not?' Not just Thoma, his father, too, had heard it. Because they had been desperate, they stayed on. All those memories would surface if he went there.

One night, when the meal was over, thinking it an opportune moment, Anna *kidathi* began, 'I want to say something.'

Thoma was lying on his back on the mat, trying to loosen his stiff and stressed muscles. He had spent the whole day tilling the hill slope.

She looked at his face searchingly. There was no change in his expression. He showed no interest in what she wanted to say. His eyes should have opened. There should have been a glimmer of interest. Nothing like that happened. Not just that, he seemed indifferent. It made her angry. There was reason for her to be angry, wasn't there? During the delicious nights after marriage, their conversations had gone on till dawn, lengthened by the sweet words that were said. Though the words were unpolished, two hearts unfurled their petals through them, to reveal each to the other. Was it wrong if she expected it to last? She was a wife. Didn't she have a claim to the rights of a wife? The husband lay silent, indifferent, as though satiated. Did that mean everything had gone stale? Truly, was it time for that already?

Anna *kidathi* asked with a wife's authority, 'What nonsense is this? I start to say something and you do not say a word in response.'

She became tearful. Her eyes grew moist; in the light of the lamp they glowed. That stirred him. Thoma sat up. As he reached out to embrace her, he asked, 'What is it my girl, tell me?'

She liked the change that took place in him. He was awake. So, if she cried it would stir her husband! That was a great thing for Anna *kidathi*. However, with that unique histrionic awareness that only women possess, she pulled back. It took an effort. It was an act. In truth, could she do it? No wife can shrug away from a loving husband's embrace.

Thoma repeated: 'What is it my girl, tell me?'

A glow appeared in his eyes, the glow of interest—proof that he wanted to know. Smiling faintly, she said, 'Shouldn't we go to my *thara*?'

He did not say whether they should go or not. But she thought his face darkened. In an instant the enthusiasm that had blossomed on his face faded. After a while he said, 'You go.'

It was enough that she go. Her husband did not forbid her from going to her house. That much was clear. However, she was shocked. What a dilemma this was! A newly wedded woman should not go to her parental home without her husband. The couple should pay a visit together or it would give rise to speculation. Would not people see it as a lack of unity between them? In truth, so few couples enjoyed harmony like theirs!

With the authority of a wife, she said, 'Why can't you come too? Isn't that how it should be, according to tradition?'

That loving wife was not arguing. She did not want to argue. She was just stating a point. She could not go to her house without her husband. A man might not understand it, but a woman knew well what the consequences would be. Everyone would say Anna *kidathi* was not a capable woman.

Thoma said, '*Edi*, your Achan is a good man, truly good. And I like him. But your Amma, she is a shrew.'

The ability to speak woke in him. Wonder where the energy came from? Somehow it happened. Her mother did not value him. Not just that, she had greater regard for Kunjol's son, Azhakan. The day Azhakan was baptized and joined the Church, it was truly a festival for Pallithara Maria. Thoma was aware of all that. Maria did not value him. He said emphatically, 'I will not come to that sort of a house. You need not wait for it to happen.'

It was a total refusal. Maybe that decision would not change. Thoma continued to talk for a long time, as though in a frenzy. Can a simple Pulayan, who walks about like a sliver of darkness, talk so well? Pride had dawned. The feeling that one is humiliated awakens the inner self; when that happens, even the illiterate can speak. He finds the words for it. Thoma talked with precision, putting forth his arguments in an orderly manner. There were no flaws in the argument. With newly-awakened energy, he said, 'Your mother might not be impressed by me. If that is so, let it be. I do not lack anything. I am like any other young Peleyan.'

He wanted his identity to be acknowledged. He was like any other young man of the Pulaya community. There was no difference. All the young men eked out their living by working for the landlords. No one had any savings. The philosophy of saving for the future did not exist in their lives. No one had taught them that. Theirs was an unadorned life that lived on the breast of the soil. The link to the soil was an ancient one. It had not begun today, yesterday, or the day before. It was a centuries-old connection. When the Pulayan turned the soil, the scent that rose from it would mingle with the air around, reach his nostrils, and intoxicate him. He inhaled the scent of the fresh soil deeply, like a rare intoxicating perfume. It was as if he had not had enough of it. An experience that knew no satiety! At that moment the Pulayan felt his body thrilling to the earth. Each speck of soil was drenched by the sweat that fell from him.

Thoma, too, was connected to the soil in that manner. That strong body demanded continuous labour. What other job should he do? When he entered the field, his powerful taut sinews throbbed with energy as he worked through the field. His songs flowed into the sky above the fields. He had strength, vigour. The creative energy that lay within him was great. When he entered the levelled fertile field with basket of seeds, the land seemed insufficient for him. He wanted to spray the seeds and bring forth a rich crop from the clay-filled land. A man who lives by this dream of prosperity will never feel orphaned in life.

To that extent Thoma, too, was content. He might not have a shred of land of his own. But was he not the true owner of all that land? If not he, then who was the inheritor of it all?

Anna *kidathi* had never imagined that her husband could become so angry. She said in a low voice, 'Why are you angry? It is natural that I should want to go to my house.'

Yes, she might feel that way. It was her home after all. She was born there. She grew up there. It was in that house that youth had embraced her, there she had savoured the sweet dreams about life. It was in the seclusion of that home that she had sat with her thighs pressed together and dwelt in the pleasurable dreams about life. She must be yearning to return to that home. It must be beckoning her. Thoma understood this but he was not willing to accompany her.

Anna *kidathi* waited for a reply she did not get. She was sad. Her home was just a few hundred yards away. She could see it from her new home. Yet, in that short space of time, she had grown so distant from it. Anna *kidathi* would see her mother from afar. Maria would look at her. Their eyes met. With a sense of guilt Anna *kidathi* would think, '*Oh, entammachi,* my mother.' But she would not go alone. That she had decided.

A mist-like barrier lay between the two houses. It seemed to spread wherever she looked. It was just vapour; yet, the inmates of neither house made an attempt to approach the other. The distance was increasing by the minute.

Outha Pulayan found this amusing. He still came to Pallithara. He chewed betel, got pleasure out of it, and told stories. Pathros and Outha Pulayan were committee members. Their friendship was a strong one, not the kind that cracks in a moment. The wedding arranged with Outha Pulayan's son did not take place. That resentment lingered. But the old man had profited. He was able to make his son toe the line, the son who till then had been living in Thakazhi with his mother. Azhakan joined the Church and became Mathai not because of any change of heart. The beautiful Anna *kidathi* had filled his eyes. That wedding would have taken place. It was Anna *kidathi* who rejected the alliance. That memory rankled. Outha Pulayan, who bore the grudge and anger of rejection in his heart, could now enjoy the estrangement between son-in-law and father-in-law. It was like mist, hardly noticeable, but it was definitely increasing.

One day, with the freedom born of a lifelong friendship, Outha Pulayan asked, '*Adi* Pathrocha, haven't your daughter and husband visited you yet?

Pathros' grew pale. Was that a question to which he could give a straight reply? No. Every atom of fatherhood in him hurt. His mind went back to the time when he used to cradle Anna *kidathi* in his arms and sing a lullaby. Were there not things to remember? She grew up. Became another's. Then she forgot the mother and father who had brought her into the world and nurtured her. All that was left now was a searing pain in his heart.

Pathros did not reply. Those tired eyes roamed the far-away skies. Some answer for this must be written in that immense vastness. One whose atoms of fatherhood throbbed could perhaps read them as well.

Outha Pulayan spat the betel juice into the yard. The spit spread like shoe flowers in the sandy yard. With increased satisfaction, Outha Pulayan continued, 'Do not think badly when I say this Pathrocha. We have to see each other again. That is why I am saying this.' He waited for a while, then said in a grave voice as though saying something momentous: 'How does one arrange a marriage, Pathrocha? We send our daughters to a home where there are relatives and siblings. We must give our daughters only to such houses. Pathrochan did not think of that. The moment you heard the young girl speak, you faltered.'

That was an accusation. A mistake was being pointed out. That it made Pathros uncomfortable was obvious. Maria came to the kitchen door. In a voice throbbing with anger she said, 'I said the same thing, *ente* Outhachaya. But this man here should listen, shouldn't he?'

Maria voiced a mother's pain. There were tears in those words. They came from a throat blocked by sobs. She was a mother. In that house there was no child except Anna *kidathi*. She had been the life of that house. The moment she left with her husband, that house fell asleep. There was no laughter, no movement. That she could bear. She had known that someday Anna *kidathi* would leave, following the man who wed her. The mother had often thought about it.

'But why can't she come to this house? She has forgotten us totally.' Maria could not control her unhappiness.

Pathros sat with bowed head, shattered, his helplessness evident.

Outha Pulayan said: 'Is that her fault? I don't think so. Maybe that young Pelen will not allow her. I think that is the reason.'

Pathros agreed. When you remembered Anna *kidathi*'s earlier behaviour, anyone would agree. She had loved her father and mother dearly. It was such a girl who had changed thus!

Outha Pulayan continued, 'That young girl is desperate to come. That young Pelen is the one who doesn't send her. That is what I think.'

At that time Maria said from behind the woven screen, 'That is true.' Pathros said nothing. He sat, head bowed; the helplessness on his face had doubled. Inside, Maria was muttering grievances, but her words were unclear. Anger and pain made them scatter and fragment.

Remembering something, Outha Pulayan said, 'I saw our Paulos.'

Paulos was first among the new Christians. He was the only one among the committee members who had some awareness. With a clear head and a body that looked as though carved from ebony, Paulos was an irritant to the parish priest and the upper castes in the Church. When the committee met, Paulos frequently asked questions. When Pathros and Outha Pulayan shook their heads tamely, and said, 'We agree,' he would disagree. His 'I did not understand that, Acho,' was a constant headache for the parish priest and Custodian Thomas. Apparently Outha Pulayan had seen him.

Pathros asked, 'And what did he say?'

Once again Outha Pulayan spat into the yard, creating a floral design.

'Paulos asked a question. Do you know what? When are we holding the anniversary of the Church?'

Pathros said with newly-dawned interest, 'That is true. Should we not have our Church's anniversary?'

'That is not it, Pathroth'e. *Nee kelu*, you listen. The anniversary is immediately followed by the election, is it not? Should we not stand for election to the committee?' Outha Pulayan explained. In truth Paulos had said a great many things. The general body would elect members to the new committee. At least four members must be from among the new Christians. In spite of having members, their rights were denied. Then what would their state be if there were no representatives at all?

Outha Pulayan expressed a vote of appreciation, 'Though Paulos criticises Achan and the preachers, there is sense in what that young man says.'

'What doubt can there be? Of course, there is.'

Outha Pulayan said gravely, 'Paulos says all three of us should be in the committee. I, too, feel that is right.'

Not just Paulos and Outha Pulayan, Pathros too felt that was right. He remembered the previous harvest. When—exhausted by the scorching sun, to ease his fatigue—he had placed a bunch of paddy stalks in his *puttil* and started to walk, Custodian Thomas had roared, 'Pathros Pelen'e, put that bunch down!' It was an order. It was the voice of a master ordering his servant, not the polite manner of one member of the Church addressing a fellow Christian. There was open displeasure and caste hatred in it. Certainly the community of first Christians was eager to get hold of the Church's wealth. The greed of the class in power, what else?

When he thought of this Pathros realized that he now understood many things. They were becoming clear. It was a feeling like that of thick mist dissolving into vapour. Pathros felt warmth spreading in his veins. They were becoming tense, taut. An uncontrollable excitement seemed to be bubbling up within him.

Pathros said as though making a decision, 'That is true. All three of us must become members of the committee. What that Paulos says is right.'

The next day Paulos came to Pallithara. He said that he had just dropped in on his way to somewhere else. But that was not true. Paulos had planned that visit.

He said in his rough voice, 'You know Pathrochaya, the Church's anniversary is nearing. There will be a general meeting, then coffee will be served. They will elect the committee for next year.'

In a clear, grave voice he continued, 'In our Church there are two groups of Christians—us, the *converted* ones, and the *early* ones. Whatever we do the two groups cannot become one.'

He paused for a moment, then said with greater force, 'We can pray and sing, and make speeches. All that is meaningless; that is how I feel each time I go to Church.'

He became even more vocal. The enthusiasm that comes on discovering a truth and explaining it, gave force to his words. Paulos said: 'Listen, Pathrochaya, don't we sing a song in Church? … That, too, is hollow, false.' Then in a clear voice he sang,

For all of us to sit together
Heaven is the same.

The song had vitality. It was melodious, because it was flowing from the Kuttanadan Pulayan's throat, a throat that had gained clarity through repeated singing on moonlit nights when the labourer drew water to drench the vast fields. The emotionless Christian song gained vigour and throbbed with life.

Once more Paulos sang the couplet tunefully and said, 'Those words are meaningless, they are lies. See, I'm just asking you because I don't know. If all of us share the same heaven, why don't we all sit on the same mat in Church?'

That was indeed a question! It was sharp, pointed. Pathros felt it pierce him somewhere. On Sundays during adoration, the new Christians sat on mats spread on the floor. Custodian Thomas and his group sat farther away at the back, where there were rows of benches with backrests. Even before God the upper castes would not sit on the floor. Their protruding bellies would not allow it. Such bodies are not meant for sitting comfortably on the floor. There was a wide gap between the new Christians and the early Christians. It was not just something that he alone experienced. It was the truth.

Paulos stood up to leave. He said, 'We'll see what happens during the election. Pathrochayan must tell all our people. I will tell all those I meet.'

In that manner, Pathros, Paulos, and Outha Pulayan would speak in each house. The new Christians would come awake. What would the result be?

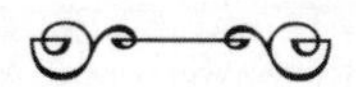

19

Life

Thoma's life changed in many ways. A new life opened itself to him, where several beautiful things locked hands and danced. A new dawn. Life gained value. It gained meaning, breadth. Earlier he had gone around careless about everything. There was hardly any responsibility. But now, everything had changed. There was a girl who depended on him. He had to fend for her. A sense of responsibility underlay the husband–wife relationship. Anna *kidathi* rested her head against his broad chest and said, 'Love me!'

Anna *kidathi* noticed the change in her husband though she did not know the reason for it. She voiced her desire to go to her house once again: 'Shall we go to the *thara*?' Her words had the meekness of a request. She could see her father and mother only from a distance. She must go to the house. She must spend a night there. She must eat a mouthful of rice served by her mother. That unfulfilled taste lingered on her tongue. So many desires!

Thoma replied as before, 'You go if you want. I will not come.'

She asked, 'Are you angry with me?'

Tightening his lips, he said, 'I am not angry,' but the voice was rough. The sweetness of love was absent from it.

Truth was, when she talked about her home, an unbearable hatred filled his heart. She said, hurt, 'My parents did not do anything wrong.'

That did not soften him. Unaffected by what she said, he retorted, 'Maybe not. But I was always filth to them.'

Once again he recalled the dark times when, having lost everything, he and his father had gone to her house and eaten their food. The expression on his face was like one forced to drink bitter medicine. He asked vehemently, 'That *thalla*, your mother found Mathai more suitable, not me, isn't that true?'

Anna *kidathi* trembled. Finally the unsaid had been said. That which had remained suppressed in his heart had come out. Her parents had preferred Outha Pulayan's son, Mathai, particularly her mother. Thoma had not forgotten anything. It seemed as though he would never forget it. Didn't men ever forget resentment and bitterness?

Anna *kidathi* had to give an answer. She had always loved him. She would continue to love him. What else could she say? With bowed head and flushed cheeks, she said shyly, 'But I loved you. Why do you forget that?'

What she said was true. He had always known it. Anna *kidathi* had always loved him, only him. He recalled how she stood sobbing on the day they were finalizing her marriage with Mathai. He should comfort her. Thoma said in a milder tone, 'I remember all that. But you must go home alone. I will not come.'

She would not go without him, she had already decided that. She would live the rest of her life at this man's feet, serving him. Even at an age when emotions ran wild, she had loved only him. She would not love another man in this life. Where else could she dwell, other than in the shade of his love?

They made some changes in that small house. A separate space was created with woven palm sheaves to serve as a kitchen. A hole was dug near the clay stove to put ash. Thoma made a shelf above the stove to store dried husks, fronds, and palm leaves. He bought a few mud pots which Anna *kidathi* arranged neatly in the corner of the kitchen. Apart from three or four clay woks, there were spoons made of coconut shells. Those were the only things in that poor Pulaya home.

The sleeping area was on the other side of the woven screen. The floor had been beaten firm and smeared with cow dung, and polished till it was dark. Thoma had stuck two cinema posters on the woven door. One had a woman looking seductively through the corner of her eye. Thoma had got it on his way back from work from the drummers who were announcing a new cinema. He brought it home carefully and stuck it on the door. Anna *kidathi* stared at it for a while. 'Does this woman have no shame?'

Thoma laughed. He said: 'Did you think all women are coy like you? Not at all. There is a young *tham'ratti* where I go to work. She is very educated. You should see the *plouse* she wears. Her entire stomach can be seen. It is that type of a *plouse*.'

Anna *kidathi*'s cheeks flushed with embarrassment. She asked unbelievingly, 'Doesn't anyone in the house scold her?'

'Why? They are all like that.' Thoma's gaze turned towards the picture—the arch look, the seductive smile. He said admiringly, 'This woman has appeared in many films. The minute she appears, there is a song, then a dance. *Ho!* You have to see it!'

He began to tell the story of a film he had seen. It was as if he was bursting to say it. A woman descends from the heavens in a chariot of clouds and falls in love with a human being. He narrated the story. He also sang a song from the film, a melodious song. It touched Anna *kidathi*. She felt herself thrill all over. She was not listening to it with her ears; to know the beauty of the song one had to feel it with the heart.

'That is cinema. It is wonderful to watch.'

'You have seen it?' she asked, her eyes widening with desire.

'Of course, yes, I have.' It was before he married her. In those days he had spent what he earned in whichever way he wanted. Sometimes he went home, sometimes he did not. But he would go to the cinema regularly. If it was a time when there was no work, he would climb one of the coconut trees on the rich and haughty Narayanan Nair's land and pluck coconuts. Narayanan Nair would say, 'He is rowdy, a good-for-nothing.'

When he recalled those days, Thoma was filled with awe and disbelief. Could things change so drastically? In those days he had been a rascal. He went about wearing a checked *mundu* that reached his feet, his hair combed backwards. There was never a time when he did not have twenty-five *beedis* and a card-mark matchbox in the folds of cloth at his waist. What freedom! His father worked in the great Narayanan Nair's field as head Pulayan. On the shelf at home stood a *puttil* full of grain. Whenever he wanted to buy something he would drop some grain onto a woven tray, sieve it, tie it up in a piece of cloth, and take it to some shop. He had wanted for nothing. That time would never return. Remembering those days, Thoma grew wistful.

'Now there is no freedom.'

A sob arose from Anna *kidathi*. Her husband no longer had freedom! He himself had said it. She was the reason for that, wasn't she? The ties of love create a unique feeling of selflessness. But her husband did not feel it.

'So I am a burden, is that it?'

She broke down crying. She had often shed tears since her wedding. The enthusiastic smile on her face had paled a bit. It should not be so. A woman wakes up when a man touches her. She blossoms. Her cheeks fill out. There is a *chethi* flower-like rosiness on her cheeks. Her laugh has the tinkling sound of bangles. A time when one who is slim like a blade of grass becomes a full-grown grain. Anna *kidathi* loved her husband, but there was sorrow in her heart.

'*Shhe!* That is not what I meant. I liked it there.'

She wiped her eyes and looked in the direction he was pointing. Far away you could see the vast expanse of Aayirampara field. The river flowed along its northern corner. The clear backwaters looked like a long broad line. A black dot moved on it, perhaps a boat. Between the backwaters and the field lay the wide outer fence. There coconuts trees stood, their branches swaying in the wind like the outspread tail of a peacock. It looked beautiful.

Anna *kidathi* understood. Her husband was a part of that vastness. It was stifling for him to live in a land full of hills, where the shade of trees fell everywhere. Life here was like that. He lived near a church, in a place covered by the shadows cast by hills and trees. There was not even enough land to walk about. One could not sing out aloud. The song that was meant to merge with the western wind could not be allowed to strike these hills. Thoma had tried to sing once or twice, but his song had lost its sparkle.

He was a son of the paddy fields of the low lands. That was where his work lay. Every minute he spent on the slopes of that hill was imprisonment. There was no changing that.

A week went by in that manner. Sunday arrived. The flush of dawn appeared on the eastern side of the hills. The birds of dawn flew about and alighted on the branches of trees.

The sound of bells from the Church floated over the calm blue valley.

Anna *kidathi* woke up early, bathed, then stepped out into the yard, her hair spread out to dry. Her husband had not woken yet. He lay on his side on the mat, cosily asleep.

A Christian must have a certain order in his life. There were certain fundamental beliefs that controlled Christian lives, weren't there? Thoma knew nothing about them. He saw a girl, fell in love. He joined the Church so that he could marry her. Wonder whether he understood that the priest had bathed his forehead with the baptism water to drive out Satan and his army? When he was being baptized he kept shaking his head like an idiot. He still had a lot to learn to live a life that was in accordance with the Church's edicts.

Anna *kidathi* stood beside him and shook him. 'Listen, wake up. Wake up quickly.'

Rubbing his eyes and yawning, Thoma stared. He sat up on the mat. The rays of the morning sun entered the room through the open door, spreading light and warmth in the house, and on the mat. He shook his head and asked, 'Why are you calling me so urgently? Have you cooked something?'

Seeing her haste, he thought she had prepared food early. But there was nothing to be seen. He was disappointed.

She said impatiently, 'What folly! All you think of is food. Does anyone have such a stomach?' She smiled fondly at him and laughed. A laugh like the tinkling sound of bangles!

'You called me just like that? Then I'm going to lie down again. There is no work today, so why not!'

Thoma lay back on the mat. Anna *kidathi*'s face became grave. The smile vanished. She looked at him like a mother looks at an erring child, 'Today is Sunday; do you know that?'

'Oh, I know.'

He felt like laughing. Did *she* have to tell him it was Sunday!

She continued, 'Look, I bathed in the morning.'

'Why?' He asked puzzled.

'We must go to Church today,' she explained. 'For God to bless us, we should go to Church every Sunday. Ammachi goes to Church. Appan too. Appan is a committee member.'

She stopped and looked searchingly into his eyes. There was no sparkle of dawning interest there. Was he going to sleep again? She poked his cheek, tickled him, and asked, 'Don't you feel like going to Church?'

'No, I don't,' he replied lazily.

Her face became solemn; she asked a grave question: 'Can we live without going to Church? It is wrong. Are we not living on Church land?'

A terrible shudder seized him. The helpless despair of the time when he had wandered about without a home returned like a nightmare. It enveloped him in a trice. He was proud of having a home of his own. It was just a tiny shack but it was his, or so he thought. That one sentence Anna *kidathi* had said ruptured that myth. That house, too, was not his own. The land on which it stood was the Church's land, was it not?

Thoma sat up. He felt faint. Was the ground slipping away from beneath his feet? In a parched, hoarse voice he said, 'Water.'

Frightened by his pallor Anna *kidathi* quickly poured out some water from the mud pot and gave him. He drank it in a single gulp. What an urge! The thirst seemed unquenchable. She asked anxiously, 'What is it? What is it?'

'Nothing.' He shook his head.

Thoma got up quickly. He took down from the clothes-line the *mundu* and shirt he had worn on his wedding day, changed into them, and said, 'Come, let's go.

Surprised, Anna *kidathi* asked, 'Where?'

'To Church. Where else?'

A faint smile appeared on her lips but she did not let it show. Biting her lip she said, 'Adoration starts only after a few hours. In the morning it is *thande kool.*'

She pointed towards the cut road that led up the hill. Young boys and girls were walking by quickly to attend Sunday school where they would enthusiastically recite the stories in the Bible. They were tomorrow's generation of believers of the Hilltop Church. How would life be for them?

Anna *kidathi* stood staring at the children. Unconsciously her eyes widened. It was a beautiful sight. The children looked so lovely, like flowers ...

She turned and looked at Thoma, her eyes filled with desire. He saw it. Thoma laughed and said, 'What is it, *edi*?'

'That is ...' She felt terribly shy. The flush on her full cheeks heightened. She lowered her dark petal-like eyelids. 'When we have children ... when they, too, go to *thande kool* ...'

Her blue-black eyes widened. A whole dream world opened up before her. What all did she see? A small life taking shape in her underbelly, the pain of bringing forth the child into the world, singing lullabies, feeding it at her breast, the beautiful child growing up. She turned her dream-filled eyes towards Thoma and asked, 'Don't you feel all that?'

Do men dream so elaborately? Only women can dream with their eyes open. But yes, he had a vague idea of family; and a child was an essential part of it.

Thoma nodded and said, 'Yes.'

Anna *kidathi* entered the kitchen area. She should prepare rice and curry. They should eat something before leaving for Church. She lighted the stove, washed a clay pot, filled it with water, and placed it on the stove. The bright red flame began to lick the pot eagerly. Anna *kidathi* washed rice and put it in the boiling water. Froth appeared in the pot, as in her heart. It boiled to the brim, escaping as steam.

Time passed. Anna *kidathi* sat lost in thought. She was imagining the moment when she would see her mother and father in Church. She thought of that moment. Her mother would place her hollow tear-smeared face against hers and kiss her. She would say, 'How could you, dear child, forget your father and mother?'

What reply would she give? Her heart would ache. She would lower her face. Could she face that moment? She felt she had acquired the bad name of a daughter who, in the joy of conjugal bliss, forgot her father and mother. That accusation rose sky-high like a mountain before her. It would not fade. It frightened her.

The red flames spread and licked the bottom of the pot, boiling fiercely, creating white froth. Anna *kidathi* sat motionless like one in a trance. Sorrow intermingled with joyous anticipation and brimmed over.

20
Being a New Christian

They walked towards the Church, Thoma in front, Anna *kidathi* behind him. For her it was a familiar world. She had been born and had grown up in a home that ran according to the dictates of the Church. That fund of experience gave her confidence. She knew to sing and pray. She also knew the stories in the holy book. But Thoma ...?

Turning towards her with a face that had not quite lost its unease, he asked, 'When does adoration in the Church end?'

She replied, 'It will take a while, it will certainly go on till noon.' With the confidence of long experience she explained: 'First they will sing a song, then the reading of one or two lines; after that Achan will speak. It will continue in that manner.'

'What does Achan speak about?'

Did she know the whole of it? The priest was very learned. Would not such a priest know a lot of things? But she had heard the speeches for so many years. Certain things had sunk into her memory in a way she could not forget. She said: 'At times Achan tells stories about Jesus. At other times it is about going to heaven. In between he frequently reads lines from the Bible.'

With newly awakened interest, he asked, 'What lines, *edi*?'

'Oh, those are all writings from the holy book.'

The couple walked along the cut road. It was a pleasant morning. Flowers hung from the leaves of trees that bent their branches over the road. Their intoxicating scent rose and filled the air. Groups of butterflies flew about everywhere, buzzing.

They climbed the steps that led onto the churchyard. The steps were made with laterite slabs laid to form a slope. Over the years green moss had grown on them and dried in the heat of the sun, giving them a grey worn-out look. A slanting casuarina tree cast its shade over the yard. Anna *kidathi* said, 'Men sit on that side. I'll enter through this southern door.'

She entered through the wide open doors on the southern side, pulling at the free end of her upper cloth to cover her head. That was the custom. Women should not display their beautiful thick hair that appeared like a poem to blackness. They must cover it, for they sat in front of almighty Lord. The Church was God's home.

Thoma stood still for a moment. Inside the Church he saw men standing in a row towards the north. Many of them held open books. Their eyes were fixed on those pages. No one noticed him. Even so he hesitated to go in. It was a new kind of life. What all would he see in that place?

Finally he entered. It was cool inside. Coloured glass pieces adorned the space above the open windows. Perhaps because of the rays of the sun falling on them from the outside, they shone with a brilliant glow. Thoma looked around. Everyone was standing. They were chanting something. He just heard the sound. He did not understand anything. It seemed as though it came from somewhere afar. He moved towards an open window.

He could feel the breeze there. It was also brighter. Thoma unbuttoned his shirt and turned towards the window to feel the air. As his eyes wandered over the universe's gracious bounty of greenery he heard the crowd say in one voice, 'Amen.'

That was a long 'Amen'. Unconsciously, he too said, 'Amen.'

On the eastern side of the large hall there was space clearly demarcated. The priest sat in an old wooden chair. Thoma watched Achan get up slowly. That was indeed a remarkable sight for Thoma. Achan was wearing a different kind of garment. Very white, a lot of intricate work had gone into its making. Oh, it had so many pleats!

The priest slowly stepped forward, then began to read loudly in a deep voice, 'The skies proclaim their creation. The earth and its colours ...'

Thoma's eyes wandered over the deep blue sky. Did it reveal the architectural skill of the almighty Lord? At that time Thoma's eyes saw something else. White cloudlets wandering across the sky in groups!

The priest returned to the big wooden chair. Silence followed. What would happen now? Thoma heard muffled footsteps from behind. Gradually they grew louder. He slowly turned his neck to look. It was Custodian Thomas, whom he had seen several times. The Custodian wore a white shirt. Therefore, the thick hairy body that lent a grandeur to his elevated status could not be seen. He had a second cloth wrapped around his neck. There was inexpressible humility on his face. Perhaps every rascal will look humble when seen inside the Church. But truly, can a jackal turn into a lamb?

Custodian Thomas walked up and stood beside the lectern placed in front. A huge Bible rested on it. He turned a page, took out a pair of spectacles from his bulging shirt pocket, cleaned it with his upper cloth, and placed it on the bridge of his long nose. Custodian Thomas let his eyes wander over all the people assembled there. At that moment Thoma saw the cunning, pompous, pragmatic man concealed behind the pious exterior!

Custodian Thomas began, 'The first reading selected for this morning: Exodus, Chapter Six, verses one onwards.' Like a child reciting with ease he read: 'Then the Lord said to Moses, "you will now see what I do to Pharaoh: Because of my mighty hand he will let them go; because of my mighty hand he will drive them out of his country."'

The reading had a rhythm. Somehow it acquired a tune as well. The Custodian continued, 'The Lord again spoke to Moses, "I am Jehovah. I appeared to Abraham, to Isaac, and to Jacob as God Amighty, but I did not make myself known as Jehova. I also established a covenant with them to give them the land of Canaan where they resided as foreigners …"'

The reading went on in that manner. Thoma listened intently. At first it did not appeal to him but gradually he became interested. It seemed to be the beginning of a wonderful journey. A forty-year journey through the desert.

When it ended the priest got up from the *maduvaha*. The people got up. Everyone began to chant something in one voice. The priest said loudly, 'Let us proclaim our faith.'

The people followed his lead and began to recite the apostle's creed. It continued like the waterfall descending from amidst the rocks, '… Believe in God, the Father almighty, creator of heaven and earth, I believe in Jesus Christ, his only son, our Lord, who was conceived by the Holy Spirit, and born of the Virgin Mary. He suffered under Pontius Pilate, was crucified, died, and was buried; he descended into hell. The third day he rose again from the dead …'

Thoma felt that he was the only one in that group who was an outsider, lonely, isolated. Somehow he felt uncomfortable. He considered going out. But he could not move his feet; it was as though they were firmly stuck to the floor. Helpless and bewildered, he looked towards the right. He could not see Anna *kidathi*. Rows of women, their heads covered with their upper cloth; how was he to find Anna *kidathi* among them? If he could see her, if he could look into those tender, liquid eyes, he would gain some relief. But that was not possible.

The priest began to preach. It was not the kind of speech that Thoma had expected, long and wordy. The priest spoke in a grave voice. He frequently called the congregation 'My children'. Thoma heard the phrase several times in the half-hour-long speech.

The priest lifted the black bound Bible with its beautiful red border and said, 'My dear children of God, this generation is full of bad deeds, treachery, and betrayal. There is no truth, no honesty.

People do not even stand up when they see the servant of God. Fear of God is totally lost.'

He raised his voice in a dramatic manner, struck the leather cover of the holy book loudly, and said, 'Therefore, my dear children, how many of us are willing to bear these holy words and follow Jesus of Nazareth, who shed his holy blood on the cross on Calvary? How many of us are willing to go out into the world and preach the word of God to the tax collectors and the sinners?'

That was indeed a question. People woke up. The priest's majestic words resounded against the heavy stone pillars of that huge Church. They echoed. The listeners began to think intensely about spirituality. Many of the women wept. They could be seen wiping their eyes with the edge of their upper cloths. An old woman at the back called out, 'Praise be to Jehovah.'

The priest stopped. He took out a handkerchief from the large pocket of his loose garment and wiped his streaming face. A circle of light shone on his increasingly balding head and then on his face. Thoma looked up. The rays came from the glass on the high eastern wall of the *maduvaha*. Achan moved to one side. With increased zeal he raised the black leather-bound holy book once again and proclaimed passionately:

'My children, Satan is like a lion roaring hungrily for prey. He is running around, eager for a prey to swallow. Particularly in these times, there is a Satan. Its name is Communism.'

The grey-haired woman shouted again, 'Praise, let Him be praised!' People exchanged glances. Women murmured. What is wrong with that old woman? Can't she keep quiet? Straightening her sari, a young woman said, 'Old woman, be silent. This is Church.'

But the old woman continued, deaf to everything: 'Praise! Praise be to Him!'

The priest continued: 'Yes, dear children, the Satan called Communism will come to each of your houses, promise to create for you a world where milk and honey flow. Do not believe all that.

What is the point if you gain everything in this world, but lose your soul? Even the learned king Solomon with all his knowledge was less than a flower.'

Thoma felt stifled. Surely, all that the priest was saying was not there in the holy book! And why was he talking about communists? Were they not trying to bring justice and equality in the society? Wasn't the priest supposed to talk about the world to come—of heaven—where the children of God would live happily for thousands of years? Thoma felt there was a flaw somewhere, but he could not identify it.

The priest became even more enthused. Raising his voice, he said, 'My children, Satan and his army will come and say many things to lead you down the wrong path. But you must not falter. You must stand firm. Only then will you gain the kingdom of God, the world of everlasting peace!'

The priest raised his hands and blessed the people. Then slowly, like a skilled actor exiting the stage, he went back to the old chair placed at the back of the *maduvaha*. A song arose. People patted their sides and got up. One of them walked among the people with a bag. Several people put money in the bag. It was called *sthothrasrisrusha*.

Adoration came to an end. A low murmur arose, as from a beehive. People began to leave. Some stood in groups in the sandy yard. Women gathered under the casuarina tree, which spread its shade, dark, like the new Christian women. The shade lengthened eastward.

As Anna *kidathi* stood waiting, her mother ran up and embraced her. It happened so quickly! Anna *kidathi* suddenly felt she was once again an infant in her mother's lap, flaying her arms and legs, the taste of breast milk on her tongue. She wept: '*Entammachi*!'

Her mother had lost weight. Surely she had become so after Anna *kidathi* left. She looked at her mother. Tears rolled down the hollow cheeks. The mother said, 'Even then, my daughter, you forgot your mother and father.'

'It is not that, Ammachi,' Anna *kidathi* wept. A thousand notes filled her throat, but she could not utter a word. Thoma stood afar. Amma asked, 'Why doesn't your *cherupelen*[1] come close?'

It was wrong. He should not stand apart like that. He should forget whatever ill-will he bore. After all, a mother is always a mother. Anna *kidathi* beckoned Thoma.

The mother asked her in a low voice, 'Does he love you?'

Truly, that question embarrassed Anna *kidathi*. The nature of their intimacy—could she reveal it? Could she transform into words that unique feeling that her soul experienced? She stood with bowed head, tongue-tied. The mother's eyes made a quick scan of the daughter. She was not the girl of old. A new grace blessed her. Her cheeks looked filled out, a blush like that of *chethi* flowers in bloom. The mother was satisfied. Her daughter did not experience want in that house. She was cherished by her husband.

Thoma came near. Anna *kidathi* stood meekly. Maria asked, 'Why don't you come to the house, *k'datha*? What did we do?'

Anna k*idathi*'s heart began to beat fast. What would be her husband's reply? Thoma, however, stood with bowed head. The fury and anger were gone. His face appeared resigned, subdued, defeated. In truth, was he not undergoing a horrible experience? He felt orphaned in that Church and its surroundings. This was not his world. His world of labour lay far away. Those fields called out to him. He could hear it with the ears of his soul. But he couldn't answer because he had become the slave of a new religion. He had acquired a new name. Oh, why did he change his name?

Maria said with a mother's affection, 'The two of you must come to the house. Do not stay away.' That mother directed a fierce look at Thoma and said, 'We do not have six or a hundred children. Just this one; remember.'

[1] Young male of the Pulaya caste.

Those words had the sharpness of a spear-head. Feeling depressed and crushed, Thoma said meekly with bowed head, 'We'll come, yes, we'll come.'

Maria pulled the free end of her second cloth over her head, wiped her tears, and began to walk down the lane, but it seemed as though a sob lingered.

Were the thick white-washed walls of the Church and the dark walls of the mud shacks symbols of irreconcilable difference?

Thoma continued to stand in the churchyard. Most of the people including Anna *kidathi* had left. You could see them going down the long lane that sloped down the hill. Thoma stood watching them descend in a line. He wanted to burst into tears. He was undergoing the harrowing experience of donning a garment that did not fit him. What great despair was this that choked the heart?

This was the first time he had taken part in the adoration in the Church, but he understood. He understood everything clearly. It would have been so much better if he had remained ignorant of it all. His heart ached. Were there gashes on his heart? Were drops of blood falling from him? The upper castes sat on benches at the back, leaning comfortably against the back rests. The new Christians sat in front on the mat, huddled together, perspiring. What a contrast! These two groups would never come together. How could people who maintained the segregation ever understand God? Singing songs, chanting prayers, and making speeches were all just charades. There was not a grain of sincerity in them. It was all a meaningless gesture, an act. There were no ideals. This was cheating. There was no piety in this adoration.

Suddenly, Thoma felt himself tremble. He was a new Christian! But what change did it create? A few drops of baptismal water had fallen on his head and Custodian Thomas gained one more slave. That was all … that was all. Something immensely powerful was flowing out of his soul; what was it? Was it an inspiration for a revolutionary act? Was all the suppressed anger within him emerging as fire?

He felt like weeping aloud. They should hear his lament, the world should hear it. They could not make him a slave by citing the name of God. Everyone should learn that. His voice should spread to the horizon and reverberate. The world should hear it and tremble. It was the voice of the new generation. They will not bear the burden of slavery. They will not make God a witness to suffer a religious belief that was built up on centuries of exploitation.

Thoma could not bear it. Were his people not realising it? They who attended Church so many times, did they not see the divide? Thoma muttered bitterly: 'They are all pigs. They just want a bellyful of food, they will be anyone's slave. Just … just pigs.'

He felt a great anger surge within him. Suddenly, he heard a voice from behind.

'Why are you standing here, Thoma?'

He turned to look. It was the noble Custodian Thomas. He approached him, his mouth full of frothy betel juice.

'Listen, *eda*, I was thinking about you. Did you hear Achan's speech today? It was good, was it not? None of you should become communists.'

Thoma remained silent. Who knew what might come out if he opened his mouth?

Custodian Thomas continued enthusiastically, 'You must lead the life of a God-fearing obedient Christian. You are living on Mission land, aren't you? Remember that and respect us upper castes.'

Thoma remained silent. The Custodian grunted and walked on gravely. Was he not a representative of the Christian family that had existed from the time of Apostle Thomas?

Thoma spat forcefully, '*Phoo*!'

He walked towards his house, feeling drained. He knew the day would surely come when he would have to defy Custodian Thomas.

21
A Storm

The anniversary of the Hilltop Church dawned. It was a grand affair. Pallithara Pathros and wife Maria, Paulos, Outha Pulayan, and all the other new Christians arrived. As always, they arranged themselves at the front of the Church on a woven mat. The benches at the back lay vacant. They would be filled by the rich, who would arrive wearing wrist watches only when the meeting was about to start.

It was a Monday. Even so, there was a good gathering. A feast that included everyone present was being prepared in the Mission bungalow.

Custodian Thomas went around supervising it all. He had no time to sit down. He would run to the Mission house, dash back to the Church; then you would see him taking four rounds in the yard thickly laiden with sand. He ran about like a caged civet cat. Yet, he never reached anywhere in time. He appeared at the Church door, his mouth smeared with betel froth.

'It is our anniversary today, is it not? I have called one or two people to speak. They will be late in arriving. Till then, womenfolk … go in and start singing.'

The dark-skinned women entered, shook the dust off the mat, spread it again, and sat down. They tugged at their upper cloths to cover their heads and the thick hair that tumbled down, like a black poem to beauty. It was the rule. A saintly disciple who wrote epistles in the Gospel had said: 'A woman must cover her head and sit silently in the congregation.' These were all rules that could not be broken. But they could sing. Shouldn't their melodious voices be used to praise God?

The women began to sing.

Paulos stood in the corner of the yard, restless. There were many things he wanted to say. There were many things against which he wanted to object. But he had not yet acquired a clear language. That would take time. Perhaps he might die and dissolve in the mud without saying anything. Pallithara Pathros and old Outha Pulayan would not believe him. They were all just slaves. They would all isolate him; that was what would happen. Should he clear the path for that?

Behold! Through the open windows of the Church, the combined sweetness from the women's throats flowed, breaking barriers. Paulos listened to the song: like granite in a pond—when you break it open, it would still be dry inside.

The song continued to rise. It rose higher and higher, vibrating with energy. It took on a life of its own; a wonderful world of God unfurled its petals through the verses. The musical streams reached their crescendo. Were the waves spreading towards the sky? It seemed as though they were flowing towards the limits of the horizon.

Outha Pulayan came towards him. The expectation of a good lunch filled the old man. On every anniversary of the congregation, Outha Pulayan would top up with a good lunch. This year, too, that day had arrived. Outha Pulayan asked, '*Eda* Pauloth'e, is the lunch ready? Everyone has to eat, *alle*?'

Paulos looked at the old man with contempt mingled with pity. Displeased, he asked, 'Achan, do you think only of lunch and eating?'

Outha Pulayan who struggled with insatiable hunger and a wrinkled body did not understand what was wrong in thinking about food. He was old. He could no longer make bunds in the paddy fields, or ply or ride the wheel. Youngsters with able hands and the will to work had replaced him. New slaves had been appointed. Those men swallowed their breakfast and left for the fields, to bend double and toil till dusk. So Outha Pulayan no longer got the breakfast he used to get from the landlord's house.

The stomach in that old wizened body churned. He asked, 'What is this, Pauloth'e, you after all have a bit of sense! What's wrong in eating the Church's lunch? I, too, give my monthly subscription and my fistful of rice, remember.'

The old man was clearly provoked. His smothered, crushed pride awoke. He had many things to say. It was the congregation's lunch he ate every anniversary. No one needs to curl the lip to give him that.

Paulos was in a dilemma. The old man had totally misunderstood him. He said, 'Achan, you flare up even before I finish talking! This is what I am saying. Listen carefully, Achan.'

In the voice of one explaining a grave and complex problem, Paulos said, 'Achan, you, myself and Pallithara Pathrochan are all committee members, aren't we?'

'True, true. All of us are in the committee, after all.' The old man nodded.

'Why were we elected to the committee?' Paulos asked sharply.

Outha Pulayan did not understand the question entirely, but it struck somewhere in his heart. He replied casually, 'Why we became committee people—because we wanted to be committee people.'

Paulos corrected him. Not just that. In truth, it was a matter that needed a lot of discussion, was it not? Paulos began to speak, his enthusiasm rising as he did. 'We are said to be committee people. Do we get to know anything? No. They, Achan and the Custodian, decide. And things happen.'

There was the priest, the Custodian and certain other members. Things happened according to what *they* thought and they wanted. There were any number of examples and past experiences. Paulos asked excitedly, 'If that is not true, Achan, just think. This anniversary celebration which is being held, did we committee members know anything about it?'

It was not just that. No decision about celebrating the anniversary was taken in the committee meeting. Then how did this decision happen? How had this meeting been organized? All these things should be done with their knowledge, was it not so? Today some stranger is coming here to speak about the Gospel to God's true lambs. The meeting was being delayed because that preacher was late. Who was it? They did not know. Shouldn't they know about it?

A light flashed in Outha Pulayan's mind. For all this while, he had been proud to be a committee member. He used to mention it to anyone he met. For the first time that pride was shaken. He thought for a while, then said, 'I'll go and ask Achan. *Ho*! We have to know this *k'datha*!'

The old man was aroused. Paulos understood this. Concealing his satisfaction, he said, 'Achan, don't go there now. That is not how it should be asked.'

The priest was extremely cunning. Paulos knew that very well. A white smile would blossom on that flushed tomato-like face; with gentle soothing words that fell from his clever tongue, Achan would easily tame Outha Pulayan. Even a tempest would be suppressed. The situation should not be one that rose like a mountain only to vanish like mist. Paulos said, 'The time for that is yet to come. Then we will ask.'

Songs resonated within the Church as their dark-skinned womenfolk sat in a row and sang. Melodious music poured into the air with rhythm and cadence. A song that could submerge all the sorrows of the material world in the intoxication of the soul; it seemed to gain life as it flowed. Paulos listened intently. So did Outha Pulayan. Were they taking in the message of the song that said that this world and everything in it were illusory? What lasted was only up there, in the world above. There the Saviour, with his pious brides, would live for thousands of years. Everlasting life and everlasting happiness! No trials, no tribulations, no afflictions.

Were those women unaware of the truth? The Church that was blessed by their vital music was filled with caste prejudice. Did they not know it? There was no light here. No spirituality. A place wholly darkened by superstition and the elitism of caste. O people, who come here hoping for light, go back! This is an organization built by rich men who have made God a witness for the prosecution. In this religion, which has turned into an organization, there is no virtue, no spirituality. It is now a dark place, where good people cannot see their way at all.

A car drew up on the main road below. A thick-set man emerged from it. Custodian Thomas ran to greet him saying warmly, 'Come, come, Saar. It is because you were late that the meeting did not start. I was a little anxious.'

The man smiled kindly. He said, 'Oh, if I say I'll come to a function or place, I will come. I'm very particular about these things.'

'Yes, yes. I know that,' Thomas replied quickly.

With the conscientious care of a guide, Custodian Thomas walked ahead, the speaker behind him. The Church could be seen above, facing the blue sky and the expanse of paddy fields. The rays of the sun fell on its whitewashed surface and cross, making them glow. The men climbed the hill. On both sides of the path stood boundaries made of mud. Tapioca branches, bent and tied together, formed fences above them. The speaker glanced at both sides as they climbed. Tiny, tiny yards all filled with tapioca, banana trees, pumpkin creepers, and ladies finger. As he looked into the whirlpool of greenery, he saw small shacks—the thatched homes of the new Christian members of the Hilltop Church congregation, believers of the true faith.

The esteemed person who had come to preach asked: 'All these huts are occupied by new Christians—yes?'

'Yes.' Custodian Thomas elaborated, 'Our sympathy for them led to them being allowed to dwell here during various times. But they all turned out to be rascals.'

'Why? Why do you say so?' the speaker asked gravely.

'Oh, what else? Rabid communists, all of them!'

It was a hint to the preacher to talk about the evils of being led astray when he addressed the congregation. But the man merely grunted. He did not give a definite reply. Custodian Thomas looked at him sharply. The preacher looked dejected. A shadow had fallen over his face. 'Wonder how his speech will be,' the Custodian thought doubtfully.

People filled the yard and the Church. The meeting was about to start. Pallithara Pathros and Outha Pulayan entered the Church. There were other new Christians too. Anna *kidathi* sat among the women on the southern side. Her husband had not come. Thoma had gone to the hill slope on the other side to clear land for planting tapioca. He had tied the *minnu* around his woman's neck and made her his own. He was determined she should not go hungry. He did not need rest.

Anna *kidathi*'s eyes swept the inside of the Church. Many of her friends had come and their husbands too. Even if one had to forgo work for a day, even if it meant forgoing a meal, one had to take part in the congregation's anniversary, and partake of the day's festive lunch. Such a meal could be had only next year. Her husband was the only one who had not come.

'It's the anniversary and you are alone, Anna *k'dathi*? Where's the man who tied the *minnu*?' asked a friend.

'Away at work.' The bride's voice cracked. The corners of her eyes grew moist. Her lower cloth was new. She wore it neatly pleated. Her upper cloth with its thin gold-border had not lost its sheen. If her husband had also come, it would have been so perfect. The shadow of sorrow flitted across her face.

She no longer looked about her. She bowed her head, pulled the free end of her gold-edged upper cloth over her head, and sat still on the mat. All around her, her happy friends were singing. The song seemed to rise and fall like waves in the sea. She listened to it. Her lips did not part. She could not take part in the joy around her.

'Achaya, who is coming to speak today?' asked one who sat beside Pallithara Pathros.

'How do I know, *k'datha*?' Pathros did not know and gestured as much.

The young man who asked the question was irritated. 'If you don't know that, why do you continue as a committee man, Achaya?'

Pallithara Pathros unconsciously bowed his head. What an insult! Pathros wanted to say something. He smarted but could not think up a retort. Yes, this irresponsible stance was wrong. It must not be repeated.

Achan entered the Church, the speaker behind him. Custodian Thomas appeared at the door on the northern side, a hitherto unseen gravity on his face.

'Let us pray. Let us pray for the Church and remember the blessings the congregation has received, the astonishing manner in which God led us this year,' Achan said.

Everyone knelt and bent forward. An unworldly peace descended on the house of prayer. Three or four seconds went by in this manner. Again Achan said, 'Now Pallithara Pathros will pray for the growth of our congregation and for the increase of God's might.'

Pallithara Pathros's prayer was well known among the congregation. No one else could pray that loud and long. Many times youngsters had become enthused by his prayer. This time, too, Pathros's voice rose and gathered volume.

The prayer was over. The next was a 'welcome' speech. The priest called the Custodian. Thomas went towards the table, cleared his throat, and began, 'My greetings to God's holy servant, reverend Achan, and the congregation.'

Paulos murmured something in Pallithara Pathros's ear and then turned towards Outha Pulayan, who shook and tidied the second cloth draped around his thin shoulders. But when he tried to rise, Paulos stopped him.

Custodian Thomas continued, 'I do not have to introduce today's honourable speaker, because he is that famous and loved by all.'

Suddenly, Outha Pulayan stood up. A powerful question shot out from the old tongue, 'Who invited this man?'

The assembly was shocked into immobility. What an insult! Achan rose and spoke in the unique voice of priestly gravity, 'Outha Pulayan, be seated.'

But Outha Pulayan did not sit down. He somehow grew brave and it showed. Invigorated by his newly awakened courage, he repeated, 'None of us committee members knew about this. Achan and Custodian Thomas brought him here. Let him speak. We will listen. But you must at least ask us before you do this.'

The visitor broke into a sweat. He looked at the priest. It was a pitiable sight.

'The decision was taken in a hurry. That is why we could not act as we should. I'm sorry about that.' Achan's tone was calm, soothing.

In such situations Achan expressed regret. If necessary, he would even beg pardon. The Pulayan could never focus or think about anything consistently. He would also soften quickly. Achan knew this very well. He began to speak conciliatory words. Paulos's question rose from the back.

'What about last year?'

That was indeed a question! It had strength. Achan was stunned. What was the nature of last year's function? It was the same as this year. Someone was brought to preach without the knowledge of the dark-skinned committee members, without their consent. Accounts of income and expenditures were presented and passed. Till now it had always happened that way. For the first time there was dissent. Where had it come from?

Achan looked at Pallithara Pathros. It was a loaded glance, a wordless request for help. Pathros leaned forward. Stretching his arm, he caught hold of Outha Pulayan's left arm. 'Achaya, what madness is this? Sit, Achaya.'

Fury blinded Outha Pulayan. The old man's body trembled. He swung his hand free energetically and roared, 'Let go, young Pelayan'e. I have to know this. They should not cheat without the knowledge of the committee members. This is a sin against God.'

Words that blossomed from the fury of the lowly ones swirled like a cyclone within the Hilltop Church. Were the stone walls shaking?

'You carry on with your anniversary. Our group is leaving,' said Outha Pulayan.

The old man led the way out. Paulos and some other low-caste Christians followed. A few women also stepped out. Anna *kidathi* watched. Her father Pallithara Pathros sat motionless. She was in a dilemma. Finally, she too went out.

In that manner the first cyclone hammered the congregation. It had great power. There was a great trembling. What were the things it would smash and scatter?

22

Paulos and Outha Pulayan

Pallithara Pathros was troubled. On the one side, there were the priest and the Custodian. On the other were his people. Which side should he join? There was substance in what Paulos and Outha Pulayan said. The present situation should not be allowed to continue. Rich upper-caste Christians dominated the Hilltop Church congregation. For a very long time they had been ruling it. Custodian Thomas's will was the law. Why?

His wife saw Pathros's distress and understood it.

'*Adi*, what is it you are thinking all the time?' Maria finally asked.

Pathros became even more upset. Maria asked, 'If Custodian and Achan get angry, let them. This is foolish! Is your fear of them greater than our own people?'

A watery smile spread over Pathros's rough face. That new Christian, who was a true believer, shook his head and said, '*Sshe! Edi*, that's not it. What our people say is true. But what will Achan think?'

Maria understood the essence of that sentence. Achan liked Pathros very much. Whenever a meeting was held, it was to Pathros that Achan turned, it was Pathros he asked to pray aloud. Achan had said several times that there was no one in the congregation who could pray with the intensity with which Pathros did. Pathros cherished that praise. He was satisfied with that occasional invitation to offer in public, an intense, inspiring prayer. Till now that man had had no complaints. Now for the first time, he had a grievance. Did that not mean that he had gained some awareness? Pathros was proud to be a member of the congregation; he was also proud to be a committee member. There was a tinge of ego mixed in his pride. That had been shattered. Achan, Custodian Thomas, and the upper-caste people were suppressing them in the congregation. His own people were mere slaves. The songs that he and his people sang within the thickly white-washed walls of the Church were all denials of truth. Those songs had no vitality. It was all just an illusion. How could the manifestation of slavery have vitality?

Pallithara Pathros was irritated. Was there anything to be proud of in his, a true Christian's, life? Nothing. He silently obeyed what the others said—Achan, the Custodian, and those who had been Christians from very early times.

As he understood that shameful truth, a change came over Pathros. His enthusiasm withered. He could no longer sing loudly, or call out 'Praise the Lord'. That old Pulayan told himself, 'Pelayan will always remain Pelayan. Joining the Church was useless—useless!'

That was a terrible revelation. Pathros thought about it continuously, obsessively. The thought lingered in his mind like sour medicine on the tongue. His heart felt heavy. Worry preyed upon it. Unable to bear the affliction Pallithara Pathros called out, '*Ente deivame*, oh my God ...'

One day Outha Pulayan and Paulos came to see him. When he saw them Pathros, conventional man that he was, felt a flash of fear. He wished he could disappear. He knew why they had come. In some unknown manner an idea had sprung up: The new Christians should unite. The upper-caste Christians controlled the wealth of the Christian congregation and enjoyed it. The poor Parayan and Pulayan had no right to it. Where did the huge income from all that wealth go?

As soon as he arrived, Outha Pulayan said, '*Eda* Pathroth'e, Achan frightened you with his words. I know that. Even so, you'll have to come with us.'

Paulos supported him. Not just that, the young man had something more to say.

'Pathrochaya, you are the big man among us. That being so, it is not right that you distance yourself.'

Pathros wanted to acknowledge that leadership. For this long, he had acted as though the leadership had been his. He had never compromised it. For the first time he began to feel that his leadership was a fantasy. By joining the Church all that the Parayan and Pulayan had gained was that they acquired the same names as the wealthy Christians and they lived with those names, nothing else; they continued to be exploited. Now the new Christians wanted him to stand with them. They acknowledged his leadership. There was some consolation in that.

Pathros asked, 'What should I do?'

Paulos was the one who replied. 'If you ask what you should do … Achaya, are you not aware of anything that is happening?'

Pathros replied guiltily, 'No, I am not.' He scratched his head as though asking for forgiveness for the lapse and asked, 'What is it?'

This time, too, Paulos explained, while Outha Pulayan nodded in agreement. 'Achan, did you not hear? Then it is very sad. We have decided to have a meeting.'

A meeting! Recalling the meetings which echoed 'Halleluiah!' and 'Praise the Lord', true believer Pathros asked, 'Who is speaking?'

Infuriated, Outha Pulayan spat out, '*Phaa*! *Ho*!' The old man continued energetically, '*Eda* Pathroth'e, listen. The thing is, our people have been cheated by Achan and Custodian Thomas. Their songs and prayers are meaningless, utterly meaningless; they have enslaved us in the name of the Church.'

Pallithara Pathros stared, amazed. He was reminded of a story Achan had once told, when he was reading and studying the Bible. Apparently a donkey had begun to speak! It was at a time when God's prophet had stood like a dull-witted man that the donkey opened its mouth and began to speak. Amazing! Even old Outha Pulayan had started to explain things!

'Why did they include our people in the Church? For what purpose? To profit from it; that was why they included us,' explained Paulos.

Paulos could not explain what the profit was. But there was something. His instinct nudged him to recognise it.

A doubt raised its head in Pallithara Pathros's mind. What did Custodian Thomas, the priest, and their folk gain from converting poor people like Pallithara Pathros and Outha Pulayan? He asked, 'What do they gain from our people joining the Church?'

That was indeed a question! Was it not right? They, the Parayar and Pulayar, were the ones who depended on the upper castes, who benefitted from their kindness. What did the upper castes gain? Nothing. Pathros laughed when he thought of the illogicality of the statement.

Paulos asked, 'Why are you laughing, Achan?'

'What do they gain?' Pathros repeated his question.

Paulos was in a quandary. That was obvious. Paulos, who bore the responsibility of explaining everything, was dumbfounded. So, too, was Outha Pulayan. He had not expected such a question from Pathros. Somehow, a swift reply danced on Paulos's tongue.

'If you ask what that is, I don't know the whole of it. But there are those who know. They are the ones who will come and speak at the meeting.'

Outha Pulayan let out a deep sigh. Paulos had brains that came awake at the right time and acted. He was relieved.

When they included Harijans in the Church, the upper castes saw some obvious advantages in it. It was not just expansion of the kingdom of Christ that they had in mind. Neither Paulos nor Outha Pulayan was capable of explaining it. They did not know enough to embark on an explaination. But that did not mean that the great secret was unknown. It was said that somewhere in their land there were Harijans who could explain these things. The very fact that there were such people amongst them was a big relief!

'Will Achan and the Custodian allow this?'

It was not just Pathros; Outha Pulayan feared the same. The meeting had to be held on the grounds owned by the Mission. Any number of people could sit in the vast sand-covered yard in front of the Church. Such a convenient place was not available anywhere else in that land.

'I, too, thought about it,' said Outha Pulayan. 'What will we do if Achan does not agree?'

Paulos was not dismayed. He brimmed with the zeal of rebellion. It had happened when he realized for the first time that he was marginalized. There sprouted within him the confidence to resist anything and anybody, the feeling that he could sweep aside whatever resistance might rise against him. Would that enthusiasm and confidence die out?

'Achan need not agree. We will hold our meeting despite that. Or else, watch out!'

Paulos spoke in a firm voice. He was confident and determined. Let Achan, the Custodian, and the dominant upper castes, all resist them. The Parayan and Pulayan who had joined the Church would hold the meeting. The new generation will resist. This was the first enactment of that great resistance. Once again Paulos declared forcefully, 'Or else you watch what happens!'

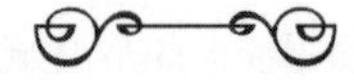

23

Paulos Addresses His People

A visible split appeared in the congregation of the Hilltop Church. The elite Christians continued to exert their customary dominance. No one resisted openly. Yet a change appeared in the behaviour of the new Christians, spreading like a film of oil on water, visible to anyone.

The new Christians still came to Church on Sundays. As usual the upper-caste Syrian Christians sprawled against the back-rests of the benches at the back of the Church. The new Christians sat on the two mats spread in front like a flock of tame sheep. The old songs continued to be sung, but they had lost their vitality. The hope and zeal in the hearts of the Pulaya women, which had once given the songs their rhythmic vitality and sweet melody, were dead. They had understood that the Kingdom of God would not arrive all that soon!

The worship and the songs dragged on somehow. Everyone noticed the pallid quality of the hour in Church. But nobody did anything about it. Somehow an issue had boiled up. It would settle down, clear up; that was all.

But Parayan and Pulayan had awakened. Everyone's goal was the meeting they had planned. On that day the people of their lowly community who had gained an education and risen in life, and who could address a gathering, would come to speak to them! They would catalogue one by one, all the injustices that the upper-caste Christians had been routinely inflicting on them for over a hundred years. They wanted to hear it, wanted to see those speakers. Old Outha Pulayan was amazed. 'In spite of everything, people who can speak a few words have come up in our community too!'

When he thought about it his greying eyelashes grew moist. The old man rejoiced to see his people progress. Did he not have the right to it? In his youth none of them had held meetings. No one had made speeches. In those days—as he ploughed Aayirampara field that yielded a thousand measures of grain, sowed seeds, and drew water to irrigate them—he had seen the landlords hold meetings. So many celebrations had taken place in Kuttanad. People came in big snake boats, sitting in rows, enthusiastically singing songs. They held meetings; there would also be huge displays of fireworks. The vast fields lay in darkness at that time. Parayan and Pulayan who had become part of that darkness often stood in the muddy paddy fields and watched the far-away lights. The sights he had seen! Many years had gone by. Now Outha Pulayan, too, could sit in the front row of such a meeting. That change was progress, was it not?

Tears filled the old man's eyes and dripped on to his bony chest. The tears were an offering to an exhilarating experience. He wept with joy.

One Sunday, adoration over, people moved into the yard. Some sat down in the shade of the casuarina tree as usual. They would sit there and tell many stories.

Paulos came forward eagerly. 'Look, we should all get together. We need to discuss something.'

Someone asked, 'What is it?'

'You ask that!' Paulos flared up. 'This is why they say our people will never prosper. We forget so quickly! Have you forgotten that we are holding a meeting?'

Someone joked, 'Why! Is the meeting today?'

'Not today, but don't we have to plan?'

The new Christians gathered in a circle. One of them asked, 'Should we not call the women?'

'Of course.'

The women stood in a group towards the south talking idly, including Anna *kidathi* and her mother. Paulos went towards them. Maria asked him chattily, 'What news, Paulocha?'

Paulos smiled. 'Doesn't Maria sister know? We are going to hold a meeting.'

Pride throbbed in those words. Other women listened. Maria said, 'I know. When is the meeting?'

Another asked, 'Who is speaking?'

A beautiful sari-clad young woman with a thick layer of powder on her face simpered, 'You should include my song.'

A bold creature!

As though she had just remembered it, a woman said, 'My younger daughter dances well. You must include her dance.'

Paulose gave a cursory reply, 'We are holding this meeting to decide what all should be included. Come, we'll all go there.'

Men and women—the new Christian members of the congregation—gathered in the shade of the casuarina tree to discuss and decide. It was a remarkable sight.

'We have assembled here for a purpose,' said Paulos, by way of introduction, 'to explain why, though we joined the Church, we still experience exclusion. The upper-caste Christians and we are two separate groups.'

A Pulayan who stood far behind, away from the group asked, 'So what should we do? Can our people and the upper-castes become one?'

Some of the conservative ones had the same question. They had not voiced it, that was all. They all nodded in agreement. The old man became more enthusiastic. Another question rose from that aged throat, '*Eda k'datha*, let me ask you something. Are we holding this meeting to turn our people into upper castes?'

There was contemptuous laughter. One or two hooted. Paulos was startled. He had expected resistance from the upper castes, not from his own people.

The ridicule acted as a trigger. Paulos woke up. He countered with a question: 'We joined the Church to be Christians, right?'

'Yes. So, what happened?'

If he were to begin to narrate the many intolerable experiences ... a long list. Paulos was once again baffled. All of them had undergone humiliation and exploitation. Were they not aware of it? Or had they all forgotten? Will they never learn anything? If so, the bondage could well continue tomorrow and the day after!

Again the question arose, 'So, what happened?'

'You ask what happened! What more should happen? Our people did not join the Church to continue as landlord and slave, it was to worship God as equals.'

That struck home. There was a sudden hush. The silence was noticeable, significant. Paulos's words had pierced their hearts like a chisel. Each one of them had a hundred painful memories to recall, experiences in their own lives. The Syrian Christians in the Hilltop Church were always '*thampuran*'. Though the Parayan and Pulayan had been baptized, they were segregated, and that continued even today.

'Friends, should we not seek a way out?' Paulos asked.

'We should,' they replied in one voice. 'There should be a way.'

That was a great moment. Paulos had won. He looked around in the exhilaration of victory. There was no resistance. Everyone was of the same mind. That was a relief. Now he could talk. He could go forward.

Paulos continued, 'Therefore, we will hold a meeting to think of a solution.' His glance swept the group once. He asked, 'Now have you understood?'

'*Aah*,' everyone nodded their heads in agreement.

Seeing someone coming along the long narrow path that led from the Church to the road below, Outha Pulayan asked, 'Who is it?'

Another said, 'That is Thoma, isn't it? Pallithara Pathros's son-in-law?'

Thoma drew near. He had changed. He was no longer the handsome young man he used to be. The time when he had thick curly hair and an ink-black body, when he wore a checked *mundu* that was not smeared with mud, was gone. He looked wild. His hair would no longer lie neatly, even if patted down. Thin and haggard, his bones protruded. Life had appeared before him in its truest colour.

Thoma sat down listlessly.

Outha Pulayan looked him over and said, 'Shouldn't you youngsters show some fervour and enthusiasm?'

Meanwhile, Paulos continued, 'There will be expenses. We should conduct the meeting well.'

Yes, we should. There should be songs and speeches. Everyone should attend, the crowd should be as thick as the flowering blue valley; no one had anything against any of this. But whom should they call to speak?

Paulos explained. Some good speakers have come up among the Harijans in recent times. Some of them are writers as well. They must be brought to speak at the meeting. A meeting had been held in far-away Mavelikkara some time ago. Paulos had gone to that meeting as a visitor. That time a young man who wrote stories in magazines had made a speech. What a speech that was! Words had flowed endlessly like a stream.

Recalling the occasion, Paulos said, 'If you want to hear a speech that is the one you should hear—I think that young man's father was a preacher.'

'Isn't that a problem?'

'*Aa*, it need not be. That young man is a smart one. People were clapping throughout his speech.'

Outha Pulayan grunted in agreement. 'That's true. I, too, heard it.'

Immediately, a man in the crowd asked, 'What is his name?'

Paulos did not know. However, there is a way, he said. Someone should go to Mavelikkara. They could send a young man who could ride a bicycle; that was enough. He would bring all the information about the speaker. There should be others too.

'Who else shall we call?' Outha Pulayan asked energetically.

'We should bring that Achan.'

'Should we?'

'We should. Now our people should make our own separate congregation. That Achan can be the bishop.'

Someone laughed. How ridiculous! A Pulayan could, at the most, be a priest, but bishop? Of course not! Even God almighty would not allow it to happen. If God's anger flared, would it not consume the whole world?

A young man with an inclination to resist asked, 'Why did you say expenses?'

'Of course there will be expenses,' Paulos said. He elaborated. They should hire lights, a mike, loud speakers, and other things. They needed to print notices. They had to arrange lunch for the speakers. There should be a bright tubelight where the women were seated. So, they needed contributions. At that moment, a member who worked in the electricity department offered to do the wiring for free.

Details of the meeting were thus discussed and decided.

Thoma alone did not say anything. He could not speak. Why did he become a Christian? He saw a girl, fell in love with her, wrecked everything to marry her. Today what did he have that was his own? Nothing; he had even lost his name. He yearned to hear the call 'Kandankora'. There was sweetness in it. It was a comfort to hear that name. No, no, he would never again savour the joy of hearing someone call him that name affectionately. Why did this name 'Thoma Pulayan' happen?

A man sitting beside him asked, 'Don't you have anything to say, friend?'

He grunted to say no and shook his head. He was a lowly Christian—wasn't it better to be dead? Those who could not accept them as human, were they the ones who would take them to the heavenly kingdom? He doubted it. Would there be lords and slaves in the heavenly kingdom too? Would God Jehovah allow the lordly Christians and the slave Christians to sit together in that heaven? Thoma thought: 'Lies ... all this is a big lie ... it was all lies.'

Everything was finalized. Now they had to elect a committee. They should get the contributions in two weeks. A notice should be printed a week before the meeting. It should be sent to the chief guest, the speaker, and a few others.

'In which press are we printing it?' asked someone.

'Does it matter? Any press will do.'

Someone suggested Thoma's name for the committee. Another seconded it. Thoma said, 'No, I can't.'

Outha Pulayan was not pleased. 'Why? It's not right for young men to stay away.'

Thoma said, 'It's not that. I can't leave the hut and go anywhere after dark. We go for contributions at night, don't we?'

Everyone understood his difficulty. Thoma's wife Anna *kidathi* was pregnant. If he went out at night she would be alone.

'We will exclude Thoma,' said Paulos.

It was a relief. But he should not abstain for that reason. He should take part in the day-time activities. If he did not join the venture, it would not be a success. Was he not clever?

'But listen, *k'datha*, you must contribute,' said Outha Pulayan. 'I will.' Thoma got up and began to walk. That he was troubled was obvious.

When he reached the hut he saw Anna *kidathi* lying on a woven mat. She was not asleep, just weary. He sat by her, pressing his body against her warmth. The warmth slowly spread to him. She opened her eyes and looked at him. The gaze was not sensual, there was affection in it. Like a mother caressing her child she ran her fingers through his curly hair. She asked lovingly, 'Is the meeting over?'

'No. They are still talking. I came away.'

'Why?'

He did not reply, but a sigh escaped him. It mingled with the air around. He stared at her belly which was growing by the minute.

24
A Child Is Born

Thoma's mind was in turmoil. He knew no peace at all. When he went out to work he was in a hurry to get back home. Anna *kidathi*'s time was at hand. She remained at home going about with her bulging belly. That thought followed him always. Was she breathless? Whenever he thought of it Thoma felt himself suffocating. He could not bear it.

It would be dark when he reached home. A tin lamp would be burning dully. In its dim light Anna *kidathi* would be seated on a mat waiting for him. The moment he entered the house he would ask, 'Are you tired?'

A pure and wondrous smile would dawn on her pale face.

That day he was later than usual. He had gone with Outha Pulayan by boat to water the eastern field. Even though they worked at it till dusk the field was not fully watered. The heads of the paddy shoots, scorched by the sun, hung wilted. How could he return without finishing the job? After all Thoma was a Pulayan, was he not?

By the time the entire field had been watered, the sky had darkened. By the time he went to the *tham'ran*'s doorstep to collect his wages, night had fallen. At a slight distance there was a cinema theatre from where the melodious strains of a Hindi song flowed out into the calm of the night. The waves of the song came and hit his ears intermittently. Perhaps the wind was blowing in another direction.

He hastened his steps. Outha Pulayan could not walk that fast. The old bones could not keep up with that speed. He scolded: 'What is this, *k'datha*? I can't run, I'll tell the truth.'

Without turning his head, Thoma replied, 'I have to reach home quickly. She is alone.'

Outha Pulayan understood. The old man asked, 'Is this the girl's month?'

'*Hmm*.'

'I forgot. Then, my *k'datha*, go quickly.'

Thoma walked faster and faster. The path that merged into the gloom was familiar. He lengthened his stride. He could see light burning in the houses beside the lane. He could hear the song of the stream as it flowed towards the vast fields. What was the stream singing?

Thoma reached the path below the Church. He looked up. There was not a single star in the sky. It was a dark night. He felt a vague fear creep into his heart. Thoma felt exhausted. He climbed the slope feeling his way. There were many pot-holes along that path.

Walking along the path that ran beside the cemetery on the southern side of the Church, Thoma found himself thinking of all those who were buried in that soil. How did people die? Illness? Childbirth?

From among the spread-out branches of the banyan tree that stood in one corner of the cemetery, embracing the loneliness, a night bird screeched. Its shrill cry pierced his ears, like the ominous cry of death. It frightened Thoma. Oh! He shivered instinctively.

He reached his hut. There was no light anywhere. Trembling, he called, 'Anna *kidathi*!'

That cry of fear fell upon the stillness of the night and echoed. It echoed loudly. He lifted the screen door and entered stooping, his heart racing. He saw her rolling about on the mat moaning softly. '*Ayyo, entammachi* … I'll die.'

Thoma trembled. The moment was approaching. The tiny human soul cocooned within her bulging stomach had begun its journey into the world.

It was a precious moment. How long he had waited for it! His patience had worn thin over the long wait. He would become a father. His heart felt warm. It called out, 'My son, my son.' Yet when the actual moment arrived … It was frightening.

Thoma prayed fervently, as if his heart would melt, 'God, ease her pain.'

He lifted his eyes towards heaven. Did God, in his heavenly abode, see it? Thoma stood sobbing. Spurred by fear, through the intensity of that fear, he was calling that unknown strange power and praying. All that time, tears fell on his breast drop by drop. They were warm.

Anna *kidathi* continued to moan, '*Ayyo, entammachiye, ente daivame*, I can't bear it.'

What horrible pain was this! The male who had contributed to that pain stood by without experiencing it. Thoma felt desperate. He could not share her pain. The creative nobility of motherhood raised her to a superior level, a height to which the proud male cannot aspire.

He struck a match stick and lit the lamp. A dim light spread in the room. She lay crumbled up on the woven mat, rolling about, bearing the terrible pain of creation alone, on her own.

Wind blew outside. The red flame of the tin lamp swayed playfully in the breeze.

It was cold. Thoma took a *mundu* from the clothes line and covered her. The cloth shrouded that huge belly, hiding the source of creation.

Anna *kidathi* said, 'Blow out the light.' As he put out the light, Thoma saw the beads of sweat on her face.

Suddenly she screamed: 'Oh, I'll die.'

The cry entered his heart like a chisel. Terrified, he asked, 'Anna *kidathi*, what should I do?'

She said, 'Go bring someone, a midwife.' She murmured, 'Or else, go home, call Ammachi.'

Pallithara Pathros and his wife had never come to his house. Thoma had never invited them. There was a reason for that. They had agreed to the marriage only because Anna *kidathi* loved him, because she stood firm in the intoxication of that love. That was all. They did not acknowledge him as a son-in-law. Her mother had preferred Outha Pulayan's son, Mathai, to him. Thoma would never invite anyone who considered him inferior.

But this was a critical moment. It was a delivery. More important, it was the first. The first delivery was always difficult. A tiny human soul was coming out of the womb into the world where light and joy played hand in hand. The body had to expand, ease up a bit. The second and third would not be that difficult because the creation that only a woman could shape would come out with greater ease. But the first was difficult and Anna *kidathi* was bearing the might of that pain alone. A woman's presence was vital. Thoma could not contribute anything in that holy moment of creation. He could only stand transfixed.

In a voice that could tear out the soul, Anna *kidathi* somehow managed to say, 'Quickly bring someone …'

Thoma ran out into the dark. The lamps in the shacks on the Mission land were going out one by one. The people who lived there were poor. Every evening they bought some salt, chilli powder, and a small quantity of kerosene oil. So, they would blow out the lamps early. There was no chance of the lamps burning for a long time.

But there was light in one house. Perhaps there was a school-going child there. As the boy leaned forward to read, the mother sat beside him, opened her betel bag, mixed the ingredients well, and began to chew. Enjoying the chew, she took a half woven mat from the shelf and start weaving, humming old Pulaya songs, melodious life stories that rubbed against Kerala's ancient history.

The old woman in the house went out into the yard when she heard the sound of Thoma's quick strides. She called out, 'Who is it?'

Thoma paused. What a relief! Someone was awake after all! He said, panting, 'It's me, Puthenthara Thoma.'

The old woman understood. Just the previous day she had asked Anna *kidathi*, 'When is your delivery?' She remembered how the girl had lowered her head shyly. The old woman moved forward. As she reached him, she asked, 'Has the pain begun?'

'*Hmm.*'

'I will go there at once. You inform her parents.'

'Then go quickly.' Thoma sped towards Pallithara like the south wind.

Thoma reached the house. A very long interval! So many things had changed. By marrying the girl who was the darling of that house, his life had acquired a certain order. He himself had gained a strong link to that home. Yet, he had never come there. Life with Anna *kidathi* was joyful. Whenever he thought of it he felt a thrill. Yet, even now he hesitated to call.

Pathros had not slept. He sat near the tin lamp reading the Gospel monthly the priest had given him. It had articles about God and about Communism. As he read the magazine printed at the Mission-owned press, Pathros was filled with awe. God was great. This world—the sky and the sun in the vast sky to provide great light during day, and the moon and stars to give fainter light at night—God created it all! He created man from mud, breathed life into his nostrils. Thus, man was made. But man walks his own way and forgets God. So God becomes angry. That great anger has flared up many times, as heavy rain, diseases, thunderstorms, earthquakes … God's anger has appeared through the ages in many other ways. Man should fear the terrible might of the Lord!

Pathros read it all carefully. The tired eyes looked up towards heaven piously. That poor dark-skinned believer looked at the heavenly abode of God. Perhaps the priest, too, was looking heavenward, lying back in his cushioned chair in the bungalow, one who praised God with a tongue that had lost the sense of taste, satiated by bread, butter, and wine.

Becoming aware of someone moving in the yard, Pathros asked, 'Who is it?'

Thoma moved into the light.

Pathros turned his head and called, '*Edi*, get up fast. *k'dathi*'s Pelen has come.'

Maria trembled. The mother knew that her daughter was full-term. Her daughter's husband, who was not on good terms with them, had come fumbling in the dark. That arrival suggested something significant, did it not? Maria understood it at once. She had given birth too, suffered the pain. Would the warmth of experience ever fade?

'Has *k'dathi*'s pain begun?' Maria asked, worried.

'*Hmm.*' Thoma grunted.

Maria turned towards her husband, 'Are you just sitting there listening? Light a torch.'

Pathros walked towards the coconut tree in the yard where dried fronds lay in a heap. He pulled out a few sheaves from the top to form a bunch and lit it. Holding the torch he began to walk. That pious man called out, '*Karthave* … Christ!' The cry came from his heart.

The small group walked towards the southern side of the Church. The entire universe lay submerged in darkness. Just a few stars glimmered in the immense sky. They were twinkling.

They did not speak. Each heart was full.

They reached the yard. Oh, what a change!

There was light there; and the indecipherably sweet cry of a new born.

Maria quickly pushed aside the screen and entered. The old woman said, 'By the time I came she had delivered, *mole.*'

The woman smiled revealing her toothless gums, a smile that spread over the wrinkles on her face. For those who stand on the brink of saying goodbye to the world, it must be a curious experience to watch new ones come to take their place. The woman had the same curiosity. The smile on that wrinkled face refused to disappear.

'It is a boy.' Maria came to the door and told her husband.

A male. Almost as if affirming the announcement, the child that had arrived into the world began to cry. To Thoma it sounded like a tender musical poem.

Pathros wiped the teardrops from his eyes. They were tears of joy. His life was lengthening. A new link had been connected to the chain of life that had begun from him. He had grown.

Thoma felt himself thrill all over. It travelled through his veins. He had become a father.

The child continued to cry. It seemed unwilling to accept the sufferings of this world. Was the cry a protest for being born into a Pulaya home, or was it proclaiming that it would not be a slave? The cry was strong. Its waves tore through the night's silence.

Thoma looked in through a gap in the woven wall. Anna *kidathi* was lying exhausted. His son lay beside her, bundled in old cloth. He was crying. That tiny mouth was open—O, so wide! The child looked like … like the tender petal of a rose!

Pathros looked up and prayed, '*Ente deivame.*'

That pious man's voice cracked. His eyes filled with tears once again.

But would true believer Pathros's God bless that child born into a Pulaya home?

25

Life Unfurls

The infant's cry could be heard from Thoma's house at all times. The whole place woke up and became vibrant. The entire atmosphere was soon soaked in the indecipherable melodious waves of its cry. Oh! Life was slowly unfurling its petals!

Maria had not yet returned to her house. Pathros went back. He visited frequently, but always went back. He had several responsibilities. He had to go to Pallithara, see that the house and its woven walls were not destroyed by termites. He had to sweep the yard. Leaves kept falling from the jackfruit tree that stood at the edge of the yard and the breeze blew them all over the place.

The old woman, too, did not go back. The advantages of having her stay with them were not minor. Those tired eyes had seen so many births. The aged woman knew exactly what to do after a delivery. She boiled *vethu* roots and bathed Anna *kidathi* in that water. However, it was Maria who bathed the baby. She placed the infant on a palm frond in the yard. As she gently pressed the contours of the nose and brow, and poured water, it began to cry. Maria swaddled it in an old cloth and placed it near Anna *kidathi*. She said: '*Mole*, give him your breast.'

At first Anna *kidathi* felt shy. How her breasts bulged! The nipples, too, had enlarged. The muscles within them were taut and heavy. Weren't those pots of elixir ready to flow for the child? She felt herself quiver and thrill all over. She felt a terrible urge to thrust the moist nipple into the child's flower-like lips. But she was reluctant to do it while her mother and the old woman looked on. How could she?

Maria scolded her, 'Don't make the child cry.'

That was true. He was stubborn. He would go on crying. Was it possible for such a multitude of notes to emerge from this tiny human being? Anna *kidathi* lifted the baby and placed it on her lap tenderly. Had she not shaped it out of life? A delicate vessel. It should not shatter to pieces.

The child's eyes were closed as it drank at her breast. Anna *kidathi* watched, thrilling all over. Was she transforming into maternal love without her knowledge? She felt like kissing the child. The mother's head bent forward. Her lips spread as she kissed that bit of gold. Only a mother can kiss in that manner.

After a while the child's mouth became lax around the nipple. Anna *kidathi* looked at the tiny face ... it looked like a rose in bloom. What innocence! Froth smeared its tiny lips. It was the milk that had filled its mouth and leaked out. Anna *kidathi* looked at her breast. There were droplets of milk on her protruding breasts.

She kissed the infant again. 'Amma's darling little thief ...'

Thoma stood watching that joyful sight. He could not have enough of it. Mother and child! Was not a heaven unfurling on earth?

Time went by.

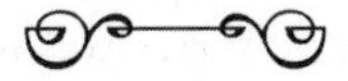

Thoma called, 'Anna *kidathi*!'

She quickly raised her face. She had not realized that he was there. A momentary bewilderment appeared on her face. She covered her breast and placed the child tenderly on the old cloth. She then got up and went to her husband. She asked, 'Why have you returned early today?'

Thoma said, 'I was watering the field. Suddenly, I felt like seeing the baby. I just could not continue. Wherever I looked, I saw the baby's eyes and face. So ...'

He moved forward, bent down, and kissed the tiny face. It seemed as if the child did not like the father's rough face. He cried. Anna *kidathi* picked up the baby and pressed him against her breast, saying, 'Look, Appan made the infant cry.'

It was a mother's voice. The mother was chiding the father. Wasn't that chiding a new experience? She quivered. She began to hum '*va va vo*'. Thoma sat leaning against the bamboo pole. A sensual lethargy came over him, enveloping his soul. He yearned to just sit there and watch that tiny bit of life that had been kindled from within him. He did not want to go anywhere. Just sit there and watch unblinkingly.

But that poor man did not have the luxury to sit idly and watch. There were a hundred expenses. His wife had just given birth, so expenses had increased. As the lone male he had to take up the spade and work. Responsibilities were piling up on his shoulders.

Once Anna *kidathi* asked in a tender chiding tone, 'Is it enough to sit watching the child like this? Don't you have to work?'

He realized the gravity of those words; he became alert. Thoma replied, as though admitting guilt, 'That is true. I forgot. When I sit watching the baby I don't feel like going anywhere.'

When she heard this Anna *kidathi* felt herself tremble with joy. Her marriage was a success. Her husband loved her. He had affection for the child that had taken shape in her womb. Not just that, he could not bear being separated from him. What more did one want to be content?

After repeatedly kissing the child, Thoma went to work. The whole day he kept thinking about his home, about the tiny bundle of life that lay near his mother, stretching his limbs! Like a tender rose petal ... He thought he saw it in his inner eye. Thoma kept smiling as he remembered it. He was unaware of the intense heat of the sun. Streams of sweat poured down his body as he stood digging on the hill slope, but Thoma's hands rose and fell mechanically. No exhaustion. No boredom. He now had a goal to work for. He had a child. It was growing. It needed food. He wanted to store in his house everything needed for its growth. In that manner a consciousness awoke. No more of the lazy careless life of the past. He was no longer the old Kandankoran who used to walk about with no thought of home, his *mundu* making a swishing sound as it rubbed against his feet, and his curly hair patted backwards. The change was remarkable. Now he went about with a clay-smeared cloth tied around his waist. His hair never stayed down, even if patted into place. And he was always in a hurry.

The days went by. One evening husband and wife sat talking in Thoma's house. A tin lamp gave out a flickering light. Anna *kidathi* had filled out a bit. There was tiredness under her eyes, visible even in the dark. But there was also brightness in them.

The child lay between them on a woven mat.

Thoma said, '*Alla,* I was thinking the same thing. What do we call our son?'

The true Christian Church had a rule. Once a child was born, it must be baptized. The priest would draw a cross on the child's forehead with holy water. Through that act the Church was accepting a strong soldier who would fight Satan and his mighty army. The child born in the Pulaya Christian's home could not avoid being baptized. He, too, should be a brave Christian. He must fight Satan and his roaring army always.

The moment the baptismal water was smeared on the child's forehead, the priest would ask, 'What will you call this infant?'

The name called at that moment was for life, immutable. When he grew up, the world would recognise him by that name. It was a serious matter.

According to tradition the boy needed to be named after his grandfather. It was a promise made by the new generation that it would remember the dying one. Thoma knew this. He said, 'We will name him after my father.'

Anna *kidathi* did not reply. She sat with bowed head. Her silence was eloquent. Her face looked serious.

Thoma asked, 'Why aren't you saying anything?'

She raised her face and looked at him. How could she express the significance of the holy act of baptism, describe its gravity? They could not select a non-Christian name. What was Thoma's father's name? Thiruvanchan Pulayan.[1] The Church would not accept that name; that was certain. Its owner was a Hindu Pulayan. That man was an untouchable. Wouldn't untouchability taint that name as well?

Anna *kidathi* said, choosing her words carefully, 'We joined the Church. Can we fix that name now?'

Thoma's face darkened. He was silent for a moment. He asked, his voice cracking, 'Why not?'

He would resist. Whether it was the Holy Church or anyone else, he would not forfeit what he owed his father. He would not allow anyone to interfere with that decision. Near the northern boundary of the vast fields, where thickly-growing *pula* palms bordered the backwaters, on the outer fence where coconut trees stood in a row spreading shade as they swayed in the wind, the elder Pulayan sits even now, with conch and cowry shells, drawing squares in the soft sand and murmuring. Thiruvanchan Pulayan. Was that name demeaning? Thoma spat, as though spitting out the Christian faith that had rendered that name lowly. His pride awoke. He said spiritedly, 'If the Church does not allow, so be it. If people protest, let them. I'll call my *k'dathan* only by that name.'

Determination echoed in those words indeed. Anna *kidathi,* who knew the danger of challenging the Church, was terrified. The other new Christians who had joined the Church would isolate them. They would not call them for weddings, would not allow them to attend burials. If one died they would not allow the body to be buried in the cemetery. The Parayan and Pulayan who did not own even a tiny bit of land joined the Church for a reason. It was not the dream of

[1] Thiruvanchan is Thevan Pulayan's real name. For the illiterate Pulayar and Parayar, it is much easier to call him Thevan. As for the high-caste folk, Thiruvanchan with the 'an' suffix is too elite for addressing a Pulayan.

going to heaven. If there was a heaven, there too the upper-caste Christians would dominate. One could not expect them to give up their dominance in the other world! Who knew that God would not take their side? No. The Pulayan joined the Church so that when he died his body would be buried in the Mission-owned cemetery. Only the Mission Church granted him that convenience.

The dream of a grave for the corpse—what other dream could the Pulayan have, he who worked himself to exhaustion every day?

All these thoughts flashed across Anna *kidathi*'s mind like lightning. She fell at her husband's feet and wept, 'Do not say that. All we have is this shack on Mission ground. We have nowhere else to go.'

26
Yearning

....

Paulos and a few others stood in the yard in front of the Church. They had gathered to put up the pandal for the meeting. Bamboo poles of various thickness and woven palm leaves lay in a heap. Two youngsters were digging holes to fix the pillars. Older people stood around, giving instructions.

It must have been three o'clock at that time. Thick blobs of clouds scattered across the sky, hoed and tossed about by the wind. As the sun descended through the mass of clouds, its rays fell on the Church, making it glow. The cross still stood tall and erect, embracing the blue sky.

Paulos said, 'Dig the holes quickly. The pandal should be ready before nightfall.'

Enthusiasm and speed increased. Every heart throbbed in anticipation of the meeting that was to take place the next day.

One among the group asked, 'Should we put up the pandal ...?'

'What do you mean?'

'Didn't the preacher say that Achan would not allow it?'

That was true. An incident had occurred. The priest had sent a letter to the preacher whom they had invited. It was Custodian Thomas who spread the news. The summary of the letter was that a few members of the Hilltop Church who did not fear the Lord were going to hold a meeting. They had the backing of the communists. The goal of that meeting was against the edicts of the Church. The Church had not sanctioned it.

Custodian Thomas mentioned this in Pillaichan's tea stall.

Similar comments were made in other places as well. As he poured hot water from the jug, Pillaichan asked, 'Though the Pulayar join the Church they are still another group. There is no link between you two groups. Then what is wrong in their wanting to hold a meeting?'

Custodian Thomas was at a loss for words. It was true that the Syrian Christians and the new Christians were two different groups. They lived completely different lives. The Church, however, viewed them as one. But Custodian Thomas could not say that. If he did, Pillaichan would immediately ask, 'Then why do you keep them apart as new Christians if the Church does not?' Pillaichan was a wily one, adept at twisting words. Everyone knew that. He might even ask, 'So you old Christians are breaking the Church's law?' If he asked such a question, it would be a great embarrassment for the Custodian.

Unwilling to accept defeat, he said, 'Let them hold a meeting. I would like to see it.'

Pillaichan asked, 'Why do you say that?'

'That is how things are. We allowed them to join the Church out of our kindness. Just because of that …'

'So they do not have any rights in the Church; that is the truth *alle*?' Pillaichan asked caustically.

'We'll see.' Custodian Thomas walked out. The wind that had been kept contained and inert within the Hilltop Church had begun to blow. It was blowing hard!

When he heard about the exchange Paulos laughed. He said, 'Poor man! He thinks he bears the Hilltop Church on his head.' His words oozed sarcasm.

Thus, an intense and severe struggle stood poised to break out in the Hilltop Church. What would happen?

By the time the fiery sun went down smearing the horizon crimson with its setting rays, a pandal had been erected in the churchyard.

It grew dark. Paulos and the others sat leaning against a pillar in the corner of the pandal, talking. One of the men asked, 'Will that young man, who spoke at Mavelikkara, come?' He added, 'It will be a shame if he doesn't.'

Others agreed. If the meeting was to be a success, that fervent young man should come. He would describe the hardship and misery in the lives of the suppressed people in words that flowed endlessly like a stream. Only then would the people awaken.

Paulos said, 'He will come. He is in far-away Ernakulam. He sent a letter saying that he will come.'

So that was certain. Paulos said, 'All that we have collected is one hundred and five rupees. We must pay for the speaker's travel expenses. We must serve him lunch. Wonder whether the money will be enough?'

A young man asked, 'Why shouldn't it be?'

'We must pay for the mike and the lights as well.'

They began to discuss the various expenses. Time rolled by. 'Hope everything goes well,' Paulos said.

Everyone shared that wish. The meeting should be grand, it should create a stir. People should come awake. It should end well.

Just then a man came climbing up the hill towards them. They saw him only when he drew near. Someone asked, 'Who is it?'

The man moved into the light. He looked frail and exhausted. No one recognized him. Must be a new Christian from some other church, they thought. The man tried to smile. It was a tired smile.

Paulos asked, 'Who are you? I don't recognise you.'

The man removed the second cloth that he had wound around his shoulder to fan himself. As he bent forward to sit, someone tore a piece of palm frond and placed it before him. 'Do not sit on the ground. Sit on this.'

The man sat down and said, 'My name is Daniel. I, too, am a member of a Mission Church.'

He began to narrate his story. He, too, had baptismal water poured on his forehead; he, too, became a Christian. He went to school, studied, and passed several examinations. He became a teacher in the Mission-owned school. But he could not continue there for long ... too many painful experiences and unfortunate events. All that he had now was the charge of a leaking tumble-down church in faraway Kuttanad. He wanted to be reinstated in the Mission school, but the priest and school management had refused. He had many responsibilities. His children were still in school. It was indeed a lucky day if a fire was lit in his kitchen!

Daniel said, 'There should be a remedy for all this.'

Paulos and others, who were deeply moved by Daniel Master's story, said, 'Yes, there should be.'

But what the solution was and how to find it was something they did not know—not possessing the knowledge for that. However, though none of the new Christian members of the Hilltop Church congregation were educated, they understood the exploitation that underlay Daniel Master's story. Of late some of their children had started to attend the English school. At least a few of them will pass the examination. A day will come when they will need jobs. At that time they would approach the priest and the Mission school management: 'We want employment.'

But they will not get a positive reply. No one had any doubts about that. The old school teacher who sat before them was a living example of the Church's indifference. That sad story should not be repeated.

The old man said in a weak voice, 'I heard you people are holding a meeting here. That is why I came.'

'What should we do?' Paulos asked impulsively.

Daniel Master had come with a clearly-conceived plan. He had many things to say.

He said, 'We are all brothers and equals in our suffering. We must send a combined written deposition to the Head of the Church, stating our grievances.'

Daniel Master explained the advantage of such an act. The indifference and discrimination that was being practised must end. When Daniel Master explained, it all became clear to them. The frustration that was frothing within each one of them acquired a distinct shape. The awareness they gained was precious. Their enthusiasm caught fire. In a voice that echoed that enthusiasm, Paulos said, 'We will write the letter. We will all sign it and give it to you.'

Daniel Master was satisfied. The dawn of hope was visible in those sunken eyes. That miserable man said, 'Is there a shop nearby where I can buy paper? We must write the request.'

Someone said, 'We will arrange all that. You should go back only after the meeting, Master. In the meantime you can speak to everyone.'

Daniel Master agreed to that suggestion. As he sat cross-legged in the pandal, exhausted, he recalled many things—the time when he heard the Gospel for the first time, how he had converted at a time when he possessed both youth and health, how he became a teacher in the Mission school, how he developed an aversion to the upper-caste Christians; there were so many things to remember. Finally his memory reached the threshold of his present day misery in a leaking, disintegrating Mission house in low lying Kuttanad.

Unconsciously a warm teardrop fell from his eyes. He sighed deeply, 'Oh, why did I join the Church?'

Painful memories were surfacing in his heart. Daniel Master directed his gaze far away towards the west. There was no light anywhere. The universe seemed to have dipped out of sight and into darkness. After a while dim lights appeared here and there in the Pulaya homes. They, too, went out soon.

Just then Pallithara Pathros came up the hill, holding a lighted torch. Paulos asked, 'Are you returning from work, Achaya?'

'Yes.'

Seeing the newcomer Pathros raised his torch and peered at him. Suddenly a look of joy spread on his face.

'Who has come? It is our Preacher Daniel, is it not? Praise the lord! When did you come, Preacher?'

The smile that lit up Pallithara Pathros's face could be seen even in the darkness.

'Do you two know each other?' Paulos asked.

'Do we know each other? Nice question.' The two men embraced each other. Soon they became engrossed in describing their lives and asking each other questions. Daniel Master asked, 'Did you marry off your daughter?'

'Yes. That, too, has happened.' Pathros's tone lacked enthusiasm. 'One who joined the Church; he became Thoma. She insisted that she wanted him. Finally I had to agree,' he explained.

Daniel Master nodded and said, 'That is good.' He sat silently for a while. He said, 'You should not feel bad about it. After all, isn't that how we all joined the Church; at different times, for different reasons?'

Pathros had to acknowledge the truth that underlay those words, however bitter it was. Unconsciously, he half raised his hand. He remembered that at one time he, too, had pierced ear lobes.

Daniel Master sighed deeply once again.

Suddenly a child came running towards them. He said, 'Achan has asked for Paulos and Pallithara Pathros. He wants you to see him immediately.'

Pallithara Pathros asked, 'Who all are there at the Mission bungalow?'

'Achan, Custodian Thomas, and some other people.'

Paulos looked at Pallithara Pathros meaningfully.

'It must be to tell us not to hold the meeting,' said a youngster.

Another agreed and added, 'What the Custodian went about saying must be true.'

In their hearts everyone was afraid. But no one admitted it. They spent some time dithering. Finally Paulos said, 'Let Achan resist us, let the Custodian resist us, we will hold this meeting.'

His words sounded like a soldier's battle call. The others gained courage from it.

'Yes, we will hold this meeting!' They echoed his words.

The words struck the walls of the Church and reverberated. It was the echo of the new generation awakening. As it struck, the foundation of the Hilltop Church shook. The tremor was strong.

Paulos and the others entered the priest's bungalow. They stood in the attractive room bathed in the light of an electric lamp. There seemed to be quite a few people there. Custodian Thomas sat next to the priest. At that moment, for some reason, Paulos thought of Archangel Gabriel who sat next to God. As he thought of it, a grin appeared on Paulos's face.

Achan looked at them closely through his shining spectacles. Then he lowered his head and sat silently. After a while Paulos said, 'We have come, Acho.'

Courage echoed in those words, the courage of a community that had become enlightened. It created waves in the acquisitive mindset that filled that attractive room.

'A command has been issued by the higher Church. You cannot hold your meeting,' Achan said regretfully.

So they could not speak about the grievances that they suffered? What other place was there where they could proclaim it all? A terrible urge to challenge sprang up within him, but Pathros controlled it. He asked quietly, 'Why, Acho?'

Custodian Thomas was furious. He said, 'Look, just look at his audacity. *Eda,* I will tell you. Your ways are against the Lord. You are going towards Satan's side. The communists here are aiding you. So ...'

He paused, cleared his throat, and said with the intolerance of the believer, 'We will not allow you to hold the meeting. It is a shame for us. And the authorities are on our side!'

Paulos asked: 'Who are these *us* and *you*?'

At last, the division was out into the open! Caste difference had been expressed openly. However much you sang and prayed, the barrier of caste continued. It would not die.

The new Christians left. The authorities had prohibited the meeting from taking place.

27
Towards a New Tomorrow

The new Christians who lived on the slopes of the Hilltop Church stood together, embarrassed and baffled. They had to hold their meeting somehow. That they had decided. But where would they hold it?

Paulos said, '*Koottare*, my people, understand this. *They* made our people join the Church.' He stressed the word 'they'.

Paulos continued to speak. He explained how the Church and the upper castes had profited from their conversion. His words sounded as if they emerged from the throat of a veteran speaker. They had vigour, they had force. Those who heard it woke up. It was as though the vibrant energy of those words was spreading to everyone around, coursing through their veins. How could it be otherwise? How could words that gained strength from experience lack vitality?

Everyone said in one voice, 'We will hold this meeting. Whatever happens we will have this meeting.' But after that it was silence. Where would they hold the meeting?

The moment he heard what had happened, tea-stall owner Pillaichan said, 'I told you before. At least now you understand.'

They nodded. They understood. They understood everything. What more was there to understand?

Pillaichan came forward from behind the tea jug. Wiping the sweat from his chest, he asked, 'So, you are not holding the meeting?'

It was that way, more or less. But they were unwilling to admit it openly. Pillaichan understood. 'What if I give you the land, will you hold the meeting?' he asked.

It was as if a blessed door had been thrown wide open!

Thus, everything was decided. The meeting would be held in the vast ground next to Pillaichan's tea-stall. It was right below the Hilltop Church. It was also decided that during the meeting a loudspeaker would be placed facing the Church. The preparations were complete.

'Should we not baptize our son?' Anna *kidathi* asked her husband again.

'No!' said Thoma vehemently, remembering his distasteful experience.

There was finality in that decision. He would not allow another new Christian to be offered to the Church. Let his son at least be free.

Anna *kidathi* asked, 'Then where will we live?'

Thoma replied, '*Edi,* I am a Pulayan. I will live in the field. I will work for daily wages. I will stay where I can, but …'

He continued with a strange vehemence that she had never heard before, 'But I will send my son to school, educate him. I will not let him become some landlord's slave. You wait and see.' As he said this, he felt something surge within him. Warm blood began to flow through every nerve. Anna *kidathi* watched the muscles on that body grow taut. He was going to sacrifice that brimming strength for his son.

Nothing could be achieved without sacrifice.

A picture took shape in Anna *kidathi*'s mind. It had clarity. The story of a journey from the clay-filled field to the bright and wonderful world beyond. It was exhilarating. With a tremor in his voice Thoma said, 'My son.'

At that moment the child who lay on his mother's breast stretched his arms. At the same time the sound of the mike arose from the ground next to the tea-stall. The meeting was about to begin. The new generation had decided to speak.

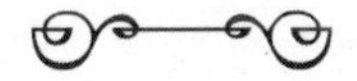

About the Author and the Translator

The Author

Paul Chirakkarode (1939–2008), born to a Dalit preacher, was a lawyer, a social activist, and a prolific writer. He has more than 20 novels, 3 collections of stories, 3 biographies, and numerous critical and political tracts in his repertoire. He also taught at various educational institutions. He was the founder editor of the journal *Padavugal*, published by the Department of Social Welfare, Government of Kerala. His fictional writings include *Nanaja Bhoomi*, *Kayam*, *Aa Velicham*, and *Puthiya Paarpidam*.

The Translator

Catherine Thankamma is a retired college professor, writer, and translator who mostly translates short stories for anthologies. Narayan's *Kocharethi: The Araya Woman*, recipient of the 2011 Crossword Award, and Sethu's *Aliyah* (2017) are the novels that she has translated. She lives in Kochi, India.